LUKE

INTRODUCTION

The Gospel of Luke presents Jesus as both the promised Saviour of Israel and as the Saviour of all mankind. *Luke* records that Jesus was called by the Spirit of the Lord to "preach the Good News to the poor," and this Gospel is filled with a concern for people with all kinds of need. The note of joy is also prominent in *Luke,* especially in the opening chapters that announce the coming of Jesus, and again at the conclusion, when Jesus ascends to heaven. The story of the growth and spread of the Christian faith after the ascension of Jesus is told by the same writer in the book of *Acts.*

Parts 2 and 6 (see the outline below) contain much material that is found only in this Gospel, such as the stories about the song of the angels and the shepherds' visit at the birth of Jesus, Jesus in the Temple as a boy, and the parables of the Good Samaritan and the Lost Son. Throughout the Gospel great emphasis is placed on prayer, the Holy Spirit, the role of women in the ministry of Jesus, and God's forgiveness of sins.

Outline of Contents

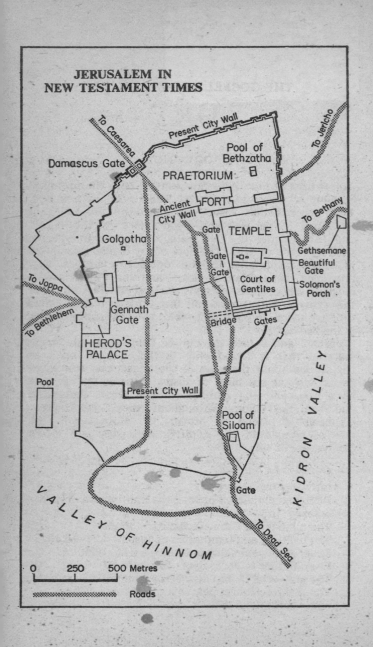

JERUSALEM IN
NEW TESTAMENT TIMES

To Caesarea

Present City Wall

To Jericho

Damascus Gate

Pool of Bethzatha

PRAETORIUM

Ancient City Wall

FORT

Gate

TEMPLE

To Bethany

Golgotha

Gate

Beautiful Gate

Gethsemane

Gate

Court of Gentiles

Solomon's Porch

To Joppa

To Bethlehem

Gennath Gate

Bridge

Gates

HEROD'S PALACE

Pool

Present City Wall

KIDRON VALLEY

Pool of Siloam

Gate

VALLEY OF HINNOM

To Dead Sea

0   250   500 Metres

Roads

1 Dear Theophilus:
Many people have done their best to write a report of the things that have taken place among us. ²They wrote what we have been told by those who saw these things from the beginning and who proclaimed the message. ³And so, your Excellency, because I have carefully studied all these matters from their beginning, I thought it would be good to write an orderly account for you. ⁴I do this so that you will know the full truth about everything which you have been taught.

The Birth of John the Baptist Is Announced

5 During the time when Herod was king of Judaea,ᵃ there was a priest named Zechariah, who belonged to the priestly order of Abijah. His wife's name was Elizabeth; she also belonged to a priestly family. ⁶They both lived good lives in God's sight and obeyed fully all the Lord's laws and commands. ⁷They had no children because Elizabeth could not have any, and she and Zechariah were both very old.

8 One day Zechariah was doing his work as a priest in the Temple, taking his turn in the daily service. ⁹According to the custom followed by the priests, he was chosen by lot to burn incense on the altar. So he went into the Temple of the Lord, ¹⁰while the crowd of people outside prayed during the hour when the incense was burnt.

11 An angel of the Lord appeared to him, standing on the right of the altar where the incense was burnt. ¹²When Zechariah saw him, he was alarmed and felt afraid. ¹³But the angel said to him, "Don't be afraid, Zechariah! God has heard your prayer, and your wife Elizabeth will bear you a son. You are to name him John. ¹⁴How glad and happy you will be, and how happy many others will be when he is born! ¹⁵He will be a great man in the Lord's sight. He must not drink any wine or strong drink. From his very birth

---

ᵃJUDAEA: *The term here refers to the whole land of Palestine.*

he will be filled with the Holy Spirit, 16 and he will bring back many of the people of Israel to the Lord their God. 17 He will go ahead of the Lord, strong and mighty like the prophet Elijah. He will bring fathers and children together again; he will turn disobedient people back to the way of thinking of the righteous; he will get the Lord's people ready for him."

18 Zechariah said to the angel, "How shall I know if this is so? I am an old man, and my wife is old also."

19 "I am Gabriel," the angel answered. "I stand in the presence of God, who sent me to speak to you and tell you this good news. 20 But you have not believed my message, which will come true at the right time. Because you have not believed, you will be unable to speak; you will remain silent until the day my promise to you comes true."

21 In the meantime the people were waiting for Zechariah and wondering why he was spending such a long time in the Temple. 22 When he came out, he could not speak to them, and so they knew that he had seen a vision in the Temple. Unable to say a word, he made signs to them with his hands.

23 When his period of service in the Temple was over, Zechariah went back home. 24 Some time later his wife Elizabeth became pregnant and did not leave the house for five months. 25 "Now at last the Lord has helped me," she said. "He has taken away my public disgrace!"

The Birth of Jesus Is Announced

26 In the sixth month of Elizabeth's pregnancy God sent the angel Gabriel to a town in Galilee named Nazareth. 27 He had a message for a girl promised in marriage to a man named Joseph, who was a descendant of King David. The girl's name was Mary. 28 The angel came to her and said, "Peace be with you! The Lord is with you and has greatly blessed you!"

29 Mary was deeply troubled by the angel's message, and she wondered what his words meant. 30 The angel said to her, "Don't be afraid, Mary; God has been gracious to you. 31 You will become pregnant and give

birth to a son, and you will name him Jesus. 32He will be great and will be called the Son of the Most High God. The Lord God will make him a king, as his ancestor David was, 33and he will be the king of the descendants of Jacob for ever; his kingdom will never end!"

34 Mary said to the angel, "I am a virgin. How, then, can this be?"

35 The angel answered, "The Holy Spirit will come on you, and God's power will rest upon you. For this reason the holy child will be called the Son of God. 36Remember your relative Elizabeth. It is said that she cannot have children, but she herself is now six months pregnant, even though she is very old. 37For there is nothing that God cannot do."

38 "I am the Lord's servant," said Mary; "may it happen to me as you have said." And the angel left her.

Mary Visits Elizabeth

39 Soon afterwards Mary got ready and hurried off to a town in the hill-country of Judaea. 40She went into Zechariah's house and greeted Elizabeth. 41When Elizabeth heard Mary's greeting, the baby moved within her. Elizabeth was filled with the Holy Spirit 42and said in a loud voice, "You are the most blessed of all women, and blessed is the child you will bear! 43Why should this great thing happen to me, that my Lord's mother comes to visit me? 44For as soon as I heard your greeting, the baby within me jumped with gladness. 45How happy you are to believe that the Lord's message to you will come true!"

Mary's Song of Praise

46 Mary said,
"My heart praises the Lord;
47   my soul is glad because of God my Saviour,
48   for he has remembered me, his lowly servant!
From now on all people will call me happy,
49   because of the great things the Mighty God has
      done for me.
His name is holy;
50   from one generation to another

    he shows mercy to those who honour him.

⁵¹ He has stretched out his mighty arm
    and scattered the proud with all their plans.

⁵² He has brought down mighty kings from their
      thrones,
    and lifted up the lowly.

⁵³ He has filled the hungry with good things,
    and sent the rich away with empty hands.

⁵⁴ He has kept the promise he made to our ancestors,
    and has come to the help of his servant Israel.

⁵⁵ He has remembered to show mercy to Abraham
    and to all his descendants for ever!"

56 Mary stayed about three months with Elizabeth and then went back home.

The Birth of John the Baptist

57 The time came for Elizabeth to have her baby, and she gave birth to a son. ⁵⁸ Her neighbours and relatives heard how wonderfully good the Lord had been to her, and they all rejoiced with her.

59 When the baby was a week old, they came to circumcise him, and they were going to name him Zechariah, after his father. ⁶⁰ But his mother said, "No! His name is to be John."

61 They said to her, "But you have no relatives with that name!" ⁶² Then they made signs to his father, asking him what name he would like the boy to have.

63 Zechariah asked for a writing tablet and wrote, "His name is John." How surprised they all were! ⁶⁴ At that moment Zechariah was able to speak again, and he started praising God. ⁶⁵ The neighbours were all filled with fear, and the news about these things spread through all the hill-country of Judaèa. ⁶⁶ Everyone who heard of it thought about it and asked, "What is this child going to be?" For it was plain that the Lord's power was upon him.

Zechariah's Prophecy

67 John's father Zechariah was filled with the Holy Spirit, and he spoke God's message:
⁶⁸ "Let us praise the Lord, the God of Israel!

He has come to the help of his people and has
set them free.
69 He has provided for us a mighty Saviour,
a descendant of his servant David.
70 He promised through his holy prophets long ago
71   that he would save us from our enemies,
from the power of all those who hate us.
72 He said he would show mercy to our ancestors
and remember his sacred covenant.
73–74 With a solemn oath to our ancestor Abraham
he promised to rescue us from our enemies
and allow us to serve him without fear,
75 so that we might be holy and righteous before
him
all the days of our life.

76 "You, my child, will be called a prophet of the
Most High God.
You will go ahead of the Lord
to prepare his road for him,
77 to tell his people that they will be saved
by having their sins forgiven.
78 Our God is merciful and tender.
He will cause the bright dawn of salvation to rise
on us
79   and to shine from heaven on all those who live
in the dark shadow of death,
to guide our steps into the path of peace."

80 The child grew and developed in body and spirit.
He lived in the desert until the day when he appeared
publicly to the people of Israel.

The Birth of Jesus
(Matt. 1.18–25)

2   At that time the Emperor Augustus ordered a
census to be taken throughout the Roman Empire.
2 When this first census took place, Quirinius was the
governor of Syria. 3 Everyone, then, went to register
himself, each to his own town.

4 Joseph went from the town of Nazareth in Galilee
to the town of Bethlehem in Judaea, the birthplace
of King David. Joseph went there because he was
a descendant of David. 5 He went to register with

Mary, who was promised in marriage to him. She was pregnant, 6 and while they were in Bethlehem, the time came for her to have her baby. 7 She gave birth to her first son, wrapped him in strips of cloth and laid him in a manger—there was no room for them to stay in the inn.

The Shepherds and the Angels

8 There were some shepherds in that part of the country who were spending the night in the fields, taking care of their flocks. 9 An angel of the Lord appeared to them, and the glory of the Lord shone over them. They were terribly afraid, 10 but the angel said to them, "Don't be afraid! I am here with good news for you, which will bring great joy to all the people. 11 This very day in David's town your Saviour was born—Christ the Lord! 12 And this is what will prove it to you: you will find a baby wrapped in strips of cloth and lying in a manger."

13 Suddenly a great army of heaven's angels appeared with the angel, singing praises to God:
14 "Glory to God in the highest heaven,
    and peace on earth to those with whom he is
      pleased!"

15 When the angels went away from them back into heaven, the shepherds said to one another, "Let's go to Bethlehem and see this thing that has happened, which the Lord has told us."

16 So they hurried off and found Mary and Joseph and saw the baby lying in the manger. 17 When the shepherds saw him, they told them what the angel had said about the child. 18 All who heard it were amazed at what the shepherds said. 19 Mary remembered all these things and thought deeply about them. 20 The shepherds went back, singing praises to God for all they had heard and seen; it had been just as the angel had told them.

Jesus Is Named

21 A week later, when the time came for the baby to be circumcised, he was named Jesus, the name which the angel had given him before he had been conceived.

Mary remembered all these things (2.19)

Jesus Is Presented in the Temple

22 The time came for Joseph and Mary to perform the ceremony of purification, as the Law of Moses commanded. So they took the child to Jerusalem to present him to the Lord, 23 as it is written in the law of the Lord: "Every first-born male is to be dedicated to the Lord." 24 They also went to offer a sacrifice of a pair of doves or two young pigeons, as required by the law of the Lord.

25 At that time there was a man named Simeon living in Jerusalem. He was a good, devout man and was waiting for Israel to be saved. The Holy Spirit was with him 26 and had assured him that he would not die before he had seen the Lord's promised Messiah. 27 Led by the Spirit, Simeon went into the Temple. When the parents brought the child Jesus into the Temple to do for him what the Law required, 28 Simeon took the child in his arms and gave thanks to God:

29 "Now, Lord, you have kept your promise,
    and you may let your servant go in peace.
30 With my own eyes I have seen your salvation,
31   which you have prepared in the presence of all
        peoples:

³² A light to reveal your will to the Gentiles
    and bring glory to your people Israel."

33 The child's father and mother were amazed at
the things Simeon said about him. ³⁴ Simeon blessed
them and said to Mary, his mother, "This child is
chosen by God for the destruction and the salvation
of many in Israel. He will be a sign from God which
many people will speak against ³⁵ and so reveal their
secret thoughts. And sorrow, like a sharp sword, will
break your own heart."

36-37 There was a very old prophetess, a widow
named Anna, daughter of Phanuel of the tribe of
Asher. She had been married for only seven years
and was now eighty-four years old.ᵇ She never left
the Temple; day and night she worshipped God, fasting
and praying. ³⁸ That very same hour she arrived and
gave thanks to God and spoke about the child to
all who were waiting for God to set Jerusalem free.

The Return to Nazareth

39 When Joseph and Mary had finished doing all
that was required by the law of the Lord, they returned
to their home town of Nazareth in Galilee. ⁴⁰ The
child grew and became strong; he was full of wisdom,
and God's blessings were upon him.

The Boy Jesus in the Temple

41 Every year the parents of Jesus went to Jerusalem
for the Passover Festival. ⁴² When Jesus was twelve
years old, they went to the festival as usual. ⁴³ When
the festival was over, they started back home, but the
boy Jesus stayed in Jerusalem. His parents did not
know this; ⁴⁴ they thought that he was with the group,
so they travelled a whole day and then started looking
for him among their relatives and friends. ⁴⁵ They did
not find him, so they went back to Jerusalem looking
for him. ⁴⁶ On the third day they found him in the
Temple, sitting with the Jewish teachers, listening to
them and asking questions. ⁴⁷ All who heard him were
amazed at his intelligent answers. ⁴⁸ His parents were

ᵇwas now eighty-four years old; or had been a widow
eighty-four years.

Sitting with the Jewish teachers (2.46)

astonished when they saw him, and his mother said to him, "My son, why have you done this to us? Your father and I have been terribly worried trying to find you."

49 He answered them, "Why did you have to look for me? Didn't you know that I had to be in my Father's house?" 50 But they did not understand his answer.

51 So Jesus went back with them to Nazareth, where he was obedient to them. His mother treasured all these things in her heart. 52 Jesus grew both in body and in wisdom, gaining favour with God and men.

The Preaching of John the Baptist
(Matt. 3.1–12; Mark 1.1–8; John 1.19–28)

3 It was the fifteenth year of the rule of the Emperor Tiberius; Pontius Pilate was governor of Judaea, Herod was ruler of Galilee, and his brother Philip was ruler of the territory of Iturea and Trachonitis; Lysanias was ruler of Abilene, 2 and Annas and Caiaphas were high priests. At that time the word of God came to John son of Zechariah in the desert. 3 So John went throughout the whole territory of the River Jordan, preaching, "Turn away from your sins and

be baptized, and God will forgive your sins." ⁴As
it is written in the book of the prophet Isaiah:

"Someone is shouting in the desert:
    'Get the road ready for the Lord;
    make a straight path for him to travel!
⁵ Every valley must be filled up,
    every hill and mountain levelled off.
The winding roads must be made straight,
    and the rough paths made smooth.
⁶ All mankind will see God's salvation!' "

7 Crowds of people came out to John to be baptized
by him. "You snakes!" he said to them. "Who told
you that you could escape from the punishment God
is about to send? ⁸Do those things that will show
that you have turned from your sins. And don't start
saying among yourselves that Abraham is your
ancestor. I tell you that God can take these stones and
make descendants for Abraham! ⁹The axe is ready
to cut down the trees at the roots; every tree that
does not bear good fruit will be cut down and thrown
in the fire."

10 The people asked him, "What are we to do,
then?"

11 He answered, "Whoever has two shirts must give
one to the man who has none, and whoever has
food must share it."

12 Some tax collectors came to be baptized, and
they asked him, "Teacher, what are we to do?"

13 "Don't collect more than is legal," he told them.

14 Some soldiers also asked him, "What about us?
What are we to do?"

He said to them, "Don't take money from anyone
by force or accuse anyone falsely. Be content with
your pay."

15 People's hopes began to rise, and they began
to wonder whether John perhaps might be the Messiah.
¹⁶So John said to all of them, "I baptize you with
water, but someone is coming who is much greater
than I am. I am not good enough even to untie his
sandals. He will baptize you with the Holy Spirit
and fire. ¹⁷He has his winnowing shovel with him,
to thresh out all the grain and gather the wheat

into his barn; but he will burn the chaff in a fire that never goes out."

18 In many different ways John preached the Good News to the people and urged them to change their ways. 19 But John reprimanded Herod, the governor, because he had married Herodias, his brother's wife, and had done many other evil things. 20 Then Herod did an even worse thing by putting John in prison.

The Baptism of Jesus
(Matt. 3.13–17; Mark 1.9–11)

21 After all the people had been baptized, Jesus also was baptized. While he was praying, heaven was opened, 22 and the Holy Spirit came down upon him in bodily form like a dove. And a voice came from heaven, "You are my own dear Son. I am pleased with you."

The Ancestors of Jesus
(Matt. 1.1–17)

23 When Jesus began his work, he was about thirty years old. He was the son, so people thought, of Joseph, who was the son of Heli, 24 the son of Matthat, the son of Levi, the son of Melchi, the son of Jannai, the son of Joseph, 25 the son of Mattathias, the son of Amos, the son of Nahum, the son of Esli, the son of Naggai, 26 the son of Maath, the son of Mattathias, the son of Semein, the son of Josech, the son of Joda, 27 the son of Joanan, the son of Rhesa, the son of Zerubbabel, the son of Shealtiel, the son of Neri, 28 the son of Melchi, the son of Addi, the son of Cosam, the son of Elmadam, the son of Er, 29 the son of Joshua, the son of Eliezer, the son of Jorim, the son of Matthat, the son of Levi, 30 the son of Simeon, the son of Judah, the son of Joseph, the son of Jonam, the son of Eliakim, 31 the son of Melea, the son of Menna, the son of Mattatha, the son of Nathan, the son of David, 32 the son of Jesse, the son of Obed, the son of Boaz, the son of Salmon, the son of Nahshon, 33 the son of Amminadab, the son of Admin, the son of Arni, the son of Hezron, the son of Perez, the son of Judah, 34 the son of Jacob, the son of Isaac, the son of Abraham, the

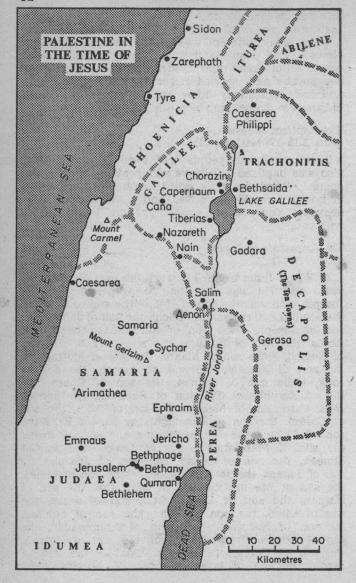

PALESTINE IN THE TIME OF JESUS

Sidon

Zarephath

Tyre

PHOENICIA

ITUREA

ABILENE

Caesarea Philippi

GALILEE

TRACHONITIS

Chorazin

Capernaum

Bethsaida

LAKE GALILEE

Cana

Tiberias

Nazareth

△ Mount Carmel

Nain

Gadara

Caesarea

D E C A P O L I S (The Ten Towns)

MEDITERRANEAN SEA

Salim

Aenon

Samaria

Gerasa

Mount Gerizim △ Sychar

River Jordan

S A M A R I A

Arimathea

Ephraim

PEREA

Emmaus

Jericho

Bethphage

Jerusalem Bethany

J U D A E A Qumran

Bethlehem

DEAD SEA

I D U M E A

0   10   20   30   40

Kilometres

son of Terah, the son of Nahor, 35the son of Serug, the son of Reu, the son of Peleg, the son of Eber, the son of Shelah, 36the son of Cainan, the son of Arphaxad, the son of Shem, the son of Noah, the son of Lamech, 37the son of Methuselah, the son of Enoch, the son of Jared, the son of Mahalaleel, the son of Kenan, 38the son of Enosh, the son of Seth, the son of Adam, the son of God.

The Temptation of Jesus
(Matt. 4.1–11; Mark 1.12–13)

4 Jesus returned from the Jordan full of the Holy Spirit and was led by the Spirit into the desert, 2where he was tempted by the Devil for forty days. In all that time he ate nothing, so that he was hungry when it was over.

3 The Devil said to him, "If you are God's Son, order this stone to turn into bread."

4 But Jesus answered, "The scripture says, 'Man cannot live on bread alone.'"

5 Then the Devil took him up and showed him in a second all the kingdoms of the world. 6"I will give you all this power and all this wealth," the Devil told him. "It has all been handed over to me, and I can give it to anyone I choose. 7All this will be yours, then, if you worship me."

8 Jesus answered, "The scripture says, 'Worship the Lord your God and serve only him!'"

9 Then the Devil took him to Jerusalem and set him on the highest point of the Temple, and said to him, "If you are God's Son, throw yourself down from here. 10For the scripture says, 'God will order his angels to take good care of you.' 11It also says, 'They will hold you up with their hands so that not even your feet will be hurt on the stones.'"

12 But Jesus answered, "The scripture says, 'Do not put the Lord your God to the test.'"

13 When the Devil finished tempting Jesus in every way, he left him for a while.

Jesus Begins His Work in Galilee
(Matt. 4.12–17; Mark 1.14–15)

14 Then Jesus returned to Galilee, and the power

of the Holy Spirit was with him. The news about him spread throughout all that territory. [15] He taught in the synagogues and was praised by everyone.

Jesus Is Rejected at Nazareth
(Matt. 13.53-58; Mark 6.1-6)

16 Then Jesus went to Nazareth, where he had been brought up, and on the Sabbath he went as usual to the synagogue. He stood up to read the Scriptures [17] and was handed the book of the prophet Isaiah. He unrolled the scroll and found the place where it is written,

[18] "The Spirit of the Lord is upon me,
     because he has chosen me to bring good news
         to the poor.
He has sent me to proclaim liberty to the captives
     and recovery of sight to the blind;
     to set free the oppressed
[19]   and announce that the time has come
       when the Lord will save his people."

20 Jesus rolled up the scroll, gave it back to the attendant, and sat down. All the people in the synagogue had their eyes fixed on him, [21] as he said to them, "This passage of scripture has come true today, as you heard it being read."

22 They were all well impressed with him and marvelled at the eloquent words that he spoke. They said, "Isn't he the son of Joseph?"

23 He said to them, "I am sure that you will quote this proverb to me, 'Doctor, heal yourself.' You will also tell me to do here in my home town the same things you heard were done in Capernaum. [24] I tell you this," Jesus added, "a prophet is never welcomed in his home town.

25 "Listen to me: it is true that there were many widows in Israel during the time of Elijah, when there was no rain for three and a half years and a severe famine spread throughout the whole land. [26] Yet Elijah was not sent to anyone in Israel, but only to a widow living in Zarephath in the territory of Sidon. [27] And there were many people suffering from a dreaded skin-disease who lived in Israel during the time of the

prophet Elisha; yet not one of them was healed, but only Naaman the Syrian."

28 When the people in the synagogue heard this, they were filled with anger. 29 They rose up, dragged Jesus out of the town, and took him to the top of the hill on which their town was built. They meant to throw him over the cliff, 30 but he walked through the middle of the crowd and went his way.

A Man with an Evil Spirit
(Mark 1.21–28)

31 Then Jesus went to Capernaum, a town in Galilee, where he taught the people on the Sabbath. 32 They were all amazed at the way he taught, because he spoke with authority. 33 In the synagogue was a man who had the spirit of an evil demon in him; he screamed out in a loud voice, 34 "Ah! What do you want with us, Jesus of Nazareth? Are you here to destroy us? I know who you are: you are God's holy messenger!"

35 Jesus ordered the spirit, "Be quiet and come out of the man!" The demon threw the man down in front of them and went out of him without doing him any harm.

36 The people were all amazed and said to one another, "What kind of words are these? With authority and power this man gives orders to the evil spirits, and they come out!" 37 And the report about Jesus spread everywhere in that region.

Jesus Heals Many People
(Matt. 8.14–17; Mark 1.29–34)

38 Jesus left the synagogue and went to Simon's house. Simon's mother-in-law was sick with a high fever, and they spoke to Jesus about her. 39 He went and stood at her bedside and ordered the fever to leave her. The fever left her, and she got up at once and began to wait on them.

40 After sunset all who had friends who were sick with various diseases brought them to Jesus; he placed his hands on every one of them and healed them all. 41 Demons also went out from many people, screaming, "You are the Son of God!"

Jesus gave the demons an order and would not let them speak, because they knew that he was the Messiah.

Jesus Preaches in the Synagogues
(Mark 1.35–39)

42 At daybreak Jesus left the town and went off to a lonely place. The people started looking for him, and when they found him, they tried to keep him from leaving. ⁴³But he said to them, "I must preach the Good News of the Kingdom of God in other towns also, because that is what God sent me to do."

44 So he preached in the synagogues throughout the country.

Jesus Calls the First Disciples
(Matt. 4.18–22; Mark 1.16–20)

5 One day Jesus was standing on the shore of Lake Gennesaret while the people pushed their way up to him to listen to the word of God. ²He saw two boats pulled up on the beach; the fishermen had left them and were washing the nets. ³Jesus got into one of the boats—it belonged to Simon—and asked him to push off a little from the shore. Jesus sat in the boat and taught the crowd.

4 When he finished speaking, he said to Simon, "Push the boat out further to the deep water, and you and your partners let down your nets for a catch."

5 "Master," Simon answered, "we worked hard all night long and caught nothing. But if you say so, I will let down the nets." ⁶They let them down and caught such a large number of fish that the nets were about to break. ⁷So they motioned to their partners in the other boat to come and help them. They came and filled both boats so full of fish that the boats were about to sink. ⁸When Simon Peter saw what had happened, he fell on his knees before Jesus and said, "Go away from me, Lord! I am a sinful man!"

9 He and the others with him were all amazed at the large number of fish they had caught. ¹⁰The same was true of Simon's partners, James and John, the

The nets were about to break (5.6)

sons of Zebedee. Jesus said to Simon, "Don't be afraid; from now on you will be catching men."

11 They pulled the boats up on the beach, left everything, and followed Jesus.

Jesus Heals a Man
(Matt. 8.1–4; Mark 1.40–45)

12 Once Jesus was in a town where there was a man who was suffering from a dreaded skin-disease. When he saw Jesus, he threw himself down and begged him, "Sir, if you want to, you can make me clean!"[c]

13 Jesus stretched out his hand and touched him. "I do want to," he answered. "Be clean!" At once the disease left the man. 14 Jesus ordered him, "Don't tell anyone, but go straight to the priest and let him examine you; then to prove to everyone that you are cured, offer the sacrifice as Moses ordered."

15 But the news about Jesus spread all the more widely, and crowds of people came to hear him and be healed from their diseases. 16 But he would go away to lonely places, where he prayed.

[c]MAKE ME CLEAN: *This disease was considered to make a person ritually unclean.*

Jesus Heals a Paralysed Man
(Matt. 9.1–8; Mark 2.1–12)

17 One day when Jesus was teaching, some Pharisees and teachers of the Law were sitting there who had come from every town in Galilee and Judaea and from Jerusalem. The power of the Lord was present for Jesus to heal the sick. 18 Some men came carrying a paralysed man on a bed, and they tried to take him into the house and put him in front of Jesus. 19 Because of the crowd, however, they could find no

Let him down on his bed into the middle of the group (5.19)

way to take him in. So they carried him up on the roof, made an opening in the tiles, and let him down on his bed into the middle of the group in front of Jesus. 20 When Jesus saw how much faith they had, he said to the man, "Your sins are forgiven, my friend."

21 The teachers of the Law and the Pharisees began

to say to themselves, "Who is this man who speaks such blasphemy! God is the only one who can forgive sins!"

22 Jesus knew their thoughts and said to them, "Why do you think such things? 23 Is it easier to say, 'Your sins are forgiven you,' or to say, 'Get up and walk'? 24 I will prove to you, then, that the Son of Man has authority on earth to forgive sins." So he said to the paralysed man, "I tell you, get up, pick up your bed, and go home!"

25 At once the man got up in front of them all, took the bed he had been lying on, and went home, praising God. 26 They were all completely amazed! Full of fear, they praised God, saying, "What marvellous things we have seen today!"

Jesus Calls Levi
(Matt. 9.9–13; Mark 2.13–17)

27 After this, Jesus went out and saw a tax collector named Levi, sitting in his office. Jesus said to him, "Follow me." 28 Levi got up, left everything, and followed him.

29 Then Levi had a big feast in his house for Jesus, and among the guests was a large number of tax collectors and other people. 30 Some Pharisees and some teachers of the Law who belonged to their group complained to Jesus' disciples. "Why do you eat and drink with tax collectors and other outcasts?" they asked.

31 Jesus answered them, "People who are well do not need a doctor, but only those who are sick. 32 I have not come to call respectable people to repent, but outcasts."

The Question about Fasting
(Matt. 9.14–17; Mark 2.18–22)

33 Some people said to Jesus, "The disciples of John fast frequently and offer prayers, and the disciples of the Pharisees do the same; but your disciples eat and drink."

34 Jesus answered, "Do you think you can make the guests at a wedding party go without food as long as the bridegroom is with them? Of course not!

35But the day will come when the bridegroom will be taken away from them, and then they will fast."

36 Jesus also told them this parable: "No one tears a piece off a new coat to patch up an old coat. If he does, he will have torn the new coat, and the piece of new cloth will not match the old. 37Nor does anyone pour new wine into used wineskins, because the new wine will burst the skins, the wine will pour out, and the skins will be ruined. 38Instead, new wine must be poured into fresh wineskins! 39And no one wants new wine after drinking old wine. 'The old is better,' he says."

The Question about the Sabbath
(Matt. 12.1-8; Mark 2.23-28)

6 Jesus was walking through some cornfields on the Sabbath. His disciples began to pick the ears of corn, rub them in their hands, and eat the grain. 2Some Pharisees asked, "Why are you doing what our Law says you cannot do on the Sabbath?"

3 Jesus answered them, "Haven't you read what David did when he and his men were hungry? 4He went into the house of God, took the bread offered to God, ate it, and gave it also to his men. Yet it is against our Law for anyone except the priests to eat that bread."

5 And Jesus concluded, "The Son of Man is Lord of the Sabbath."

The Man with a Paralysed Hand
(Matt. 12.9-14; Mark 3.1-6)

6 On another Sabbath Jesus went into a synagogue and taught. A man was there whose right hand was paralysed. 7Some teachers of the Law and some Pharisees wanted a reason to accuse Jesus of doing wrong, so they watched him closely to see if he would heal on the Sabbath. 8But Jesus knew their thoughts and said to the man, "Stand up and come here to the front." The man got up and stood there. 9Then Jesus said to them, "I ask you: What does our Law allow us to do on the Sabbath? To help or to harm? To save a man's life or destroy it?" 10He looked around

at them all; then he said^d to the man, "Stretch out your hand." He did so, and his hand became well again.

11 They were filled with rage and began to discuss among themselves what they could do to Jesus.

Jesus Chooses the Twelve Apostles
(Matt. 10.1-4; Mark 3.13-19)

12 At that time Jesus went up a hill to pray and spent the whole night there praying to God. 13 When day came, he called his disciples to him and chose twelve of them, whom he named apostles: 14 Simon (whom he named Peter) and his brother Andrew; James and John, Philip and Bartholomew, 15 Matthew and Thomas, James son of Alphaeus, and Simon (who was called the Patriot), 16 Judas son of James, and Judas Iscariot, who became the traitor.

Jesus Teaches and Heals
(Matt. 4.23-25)

17 When Jesus had come down from the hill with the apostles, he stood on a level place with a large number of his disciples. A large crowd of people was there from all over Judaea and from Jerusalem and from the coastal cities of Tyre and Sidon; 18 they had come to hear him and to be healed of their diseases. Those who were troubled by evil spirits also came and were healed. 19 All the people tried to touch him, for power was going out from him and healing them all.

Happiness and Sorrow
(Matt. 5.1-12)

20 Jesus looked at his disciples and said,
"Happy are you poor;
   the Kingdom of God is yours!
21 "Happy are you who are hungry now;
   you will be filled!
"Happy are you who weep now;
   you will laugh!
22 "Happy are you when people hate you, reject

---

^{d}said; *some manuscripts have* said angrily.

you, insult you, and say that you are evil, all because of the Son of Man! 23 Be glad when that happens, and dance for joy, because a great reward is kept for you in heaven. For their ancestors did the very same things to the prophets.

24 "But how terrible for you who are rich now;
    you have had your easy life!

25 "How terrible for you who are full now;
    you will go hungry!

"How terrible for you who laugh now;
    you will mourn and weep!

26 "How terrible when all people speak well of you; their ancestors said the very same things about the false prophets.

Love for Enemies
(Matt. 5.38–48; 7.12a)

27 "But I tell you who hear me: Love your enemies, do good to those who hate you, 28 bless those who curse you, and pray for those who ill-treat you. 29 If anyone hits you on one cheek, let him hit the other one too; if someone takes your coat, let him have your shirt as well. 30 Give to everyone who asks you for something, and when someone takes what is yours, do not ask for it back. 31 Do for others just what you want them to do for you.

32 "If you love only the people who love you, why should you receive a blessing? Even sinners love those who love them! 33 And if you do good only to those who do good to you, why should you receive a blessing? Even sinners do that! 34 And if you lend only to those from whom you hope to get it back, why should you receive a blessing? Even sinners lend to sinners, to get back the same amount! 35 No! Love your enemies and do good to them; lend and expect nothing back. You will then have a great reward, and you will be sons of the Most High God. For he is good to the ungrateful and the wicked. 36 Be merciful just as your Father is merciful.

Judging Others
(Matt. 7.1–5)

37 "Do not judge others, and God will not judge

you; do not condemn others, and God will not condemn you; forgive others, and God will forgive you. 38 Give to others, and God will give to you. Indeed, you will receive a full measure, a generous helping, poured into your hands—all that you can hold. The measure you use for others is the one that God will use for you."

39 And Jesus told them this parable: "One blind man cannot lead another one; if he does, both will fall into a ditch. 40 No pupil is greater than his teacher; but every pupil, when he has completed his training, will be like his teacher.

41 "Why do you look at the speck in your brother's eye, but pay no attention to the log in your own eye? 42 How can you say to your brother, 'Please, brother, let me take that speck out of your eye,' yet cannot even see the log in your own eye? You hypocrite! First take the log out of your own eye, and then you will be able to see clearly to take the speck out of your brother's eye.

A Tree and Its Fruit
(Matt. 7.16-20; 12.33-35)

43 "A healthy tree does not bear bad fruit, nor does a poor tree bear good fruit. 44 Every tree is known by the fruit it bears; you do not pick figs from thorn bushes or gather grapes from bramble bushes. 45 A good person brings good out of the treasure of good things in his heart; a bad person brings bad out of his treasure of bad things. For the mouth speaks what the heart is full of.

The Two House Builders
(Matt. 7.24-27)

46 "Why do you call me, 'Lord, Lord,' and yet don't do what I tell you? 47 Anyone who comes to me and listens to my words and obeys them—I will show you what he is like. 48 He is like a man who, in building his house, dug deep and laid the foundation on rock. The river overflowed and hit that house but could not shake it, because it was well built. 49 But anyone who hears my words and does not obey them is like a man who built his house without laying

a foundation; when the flood hit that house it fell at once—and what a terrible crash that was!"

Jesus Heals a Roman Officer's Servant
(Matt. 8.5–13)

7 When Jesus had finished saying all these things to the people, he went to Capernaum. ²A Roman officer there had a servant who was very dear to him; the man was sick and about to die. ³When the officer heard about Jesus, he sent some Jewish elders to ask him to come and heal his servant. ⁴They came to Jesus and begged him earnestly, "This man really deserves your help. ⁵He loves our people and he himself built a synagogue for us."

6 So Jesus went with them. He was not far from the house when the officer sent friends to tell him, "Sir, don't trouble yourself. I do not deserve to have you come into my house, ⁷neither do I consider myself worthy to come to you in person. Just give the order, and my servant will get well. ⁸I, too, am a man placed under the authority of superior officers, and I have soldiers under me. I order this one, 'Go!' and he goes; I order that one, 'Come!' and he comes; and I order my slave, 'Do this!' and he does it."

9 Jesus was surprised when he heard this; he turned round and said to the crowd following him, "I tell you, I have never found faith like this, not even in Israel!"

10 The messengers went back to the officer's house and found his servant well.

Jesus Raises a Widow's Son

11 Soon afterwards^e Jesus went to a town called Nain, accompanied by his disciples and a large crowd. ¹²Just as he arrived at the gate of the town, a funeral procession was coming out. The dead man was the only son of a woman who was a widow, and a large crowd from the town was with her. ¹³When the Lord saw her, his heart was filled with pity for her, and he said to her, "Don't cry." ¹⁴Then he walked over and touched the coffin, and the men carrying it

---

^e Soon afterwards; *some manuscripts have* The next day.

stopped. Jesus said, "Young man! Get up, I tell you!" [15] The dead man sat up and began to talk, and Jesus gave him back to his mother.

16 They all were filled with fear and praised God. "A great prophet has appeared among us!" they said; "God has come to save his people!"

17 This news about Jesus went out through all the country and the surrounding territory.

The Messengers from John the Baptist
(Matt. 11.2–19)

18 When John's disciples told him about all these things, he called two of them [19] and sent them to the Lord to ask him, "Are you the one John said was going to come, or should we expect someone else?"

20 When they came to Jesus, they said, "John the Baptist sent us to ask if you are the one he said was going to come, or if we should expect someone else."

21 At that very time Jesus cured many people of their sicknesses, diseases, and evil spirits, and gave sight to many blind people. [22] He answered John's messengers, "Go back and tell John what you have seen and heard: the blind can see, the lame can walk, those who suffer from dreaded skin-diseases are made clean,f the deaf can hear, the dead are raised to life, and the Good News is preached to the poor. [23] How happy are those who have no doubts about me!"

24 After John's messengers had left, Jesus began to speak about him to the crowds: "When you went out to John in the desert, what did you expect to see? A blade of grass bending in the wind? [25] What did you go out to see? A man dressed up in fancy clothes? People who dress like that and live in luxury are found in palaces! [26] Tell me, what did you go out to see? A prophet? Yes indeed, but you saw much more than a prophet. [27] For John is the one of whom the scripture says: 'God said, I will send my messenger ahead of you to open the way for

---

fMADE CLEAN: *See 5.12.*

you.' 28I tell you," Jesus added, "John is greater than any man who has ever lived. But he who is least in the Kingdom of God is greater than John."

29 All the people heard him; they and especially the tax collectors were the ones who had obeyed God's righteous demands and had been baptized by John. 30But the Pharisees and the teachers of the Law rejected God's purpose for themselves and refused to be baptized by John.

31 Jesus continued, "Now to what can I compare the people of this day? What are they like? 32They are like children sitting in the market-place. One group shouts to the other, 'We played wedding music for you, but you wouldn't dance! We sang funeral songs, but you wouldn't cry!' 33John the Baptist came, and he fasted and drank no wine, and you said, 'He has a demon in him!' 34The Son of Man came, and he ate and drank, and you said, 'Look at this man! He is a glutton and a drinker, a friend of tax collectors and other outcasts!' 35God's wisdom, however, is shown to be true by all who accept it."

Jesus at the Home of Simon the Pharisee

36 A Pharisee invited Jesus to have dinner with him, and Jesus went to his house and sat down to eat. 37In that town was a woman who lived a sinful life. She heard that Jesus was eating in the Pharisee's house, so she brought an alabaster jar full of perfume 38and stood behind Jesus, by his feet, crying and wetting his feet with her tears. Then she dried his feet with her hair, kissed them, and poured the perfume on them. 39When the Pharisee saw this, he said to himself, "If this man really were a prophet, he would know who this woman is who is touching him; he would know what kind of sinful life she lives!"

40 Jesus spoke up and said to him, "Simon, I have something to tell you."

"Yes, Teacher," he said, "tell me."

41 "There were two men who owed money to a moneylender," Jesus began. "One owed him five hundred silver coins, and the other one fifty. 42Neither of them could pay him back, so he cancelled the debts of both. Which one, then, will love him more?"

43 "I suppose," answered Simon, "that it would be the one who was forgiven more."

"You are right," said Jesus. 44 Then he turned to the woman and said to Simon, "Do you see this woman? I came into your home, and you gave me no water for my feet, but she has washed my feet with her tears and dried them with her hair. 45 You did not welcome me with a kiss, but she has not stopped kissing my feet since I came. 46 You provided no olive-oil for my head, but she has covered my feet with perfume. 47 I tell you, then, the great love she has shown proves that her many sins have been forgiven. But whoever has been forgiven little shows only a little love."

48 Then Jesus said to the woman, "Your sins are forgiven."

49 The others sitting at the table began to say to themselves, "Who is this, who even forgives sins?"

50 But Jesus said to the woman, "Your faith has saved you; go in peace."

Women Who Accompanied Jesus

8 Some time later Jesus travelled through towns and villages, preaching the Good News about the Kingdom of God. The twelve disciples went with him, 2 and so did some women who had been healed of evil spirits and diseases: Mary (who was called Magdalene), from whom seven demons had been driven out; 3 Joanna, whose husband Chuza was an officer in Herod's court; and Susanna, and many other women who used their own resources to help Jesus and his disciples.

The Parable of the Sower
(Matt. 13.1–9; Mark 4.1–9)

4 People kept coming to Jesus from one town after another; and when a great crowd gathered, Jesus told this parable:

5 "Once there was a man who went out to sow corn. As he scattered the seed in the field, some of it fell along the path, where it was stepped on, and the birds ate it up. 6 Some of it fell on rocky ground, and when the plants sprouted, they dried up

because the soil had no moisture. ⁷Some of the seed
fell among thorn bushes, which grew up with the
plants and choked them. ⁸And some seeds fell in
good soil; the plants grew and produced corn, a hundred grains each."

And Jesus concluded, "Listen, then, if you have
ears!"

The Purpose of the Parables
(Matt. 13.10–17; Mark 4.10–12)

9 His disciples asked Jesus what this parable meant,
¹⁰and he answered, "The knowledge of the secrets
of the Kingdom of God has been given to you, but
to the rest it comes by means of parables, so that
they may look but not see, and listen but not understand.

Jesus Explains the Parable of the Sower
(Matt. 13.18–23; Mark 4.13–20)

11 "This is what the parable means: the seed is
the word of God. ¹²The seeds that fell along the
path stand for those who hear; but the Devil comes
and takes the message away from their hearts in
order to keep them from believing and being saved.
¹³The seeds that fell on rocky ground stand for those
who hear the message and receive it gladly. But it
does not sink deep into them; they believe only for a
while but when the time of testing comes, they fall
away. ¹⁴The seeds that fell among thorn bushes stand
for those who hear; but the worries and riches and
pleasures of this life crowd in and choke them, and
their fruit never ripens. ¹⁵The seeds that fell in good
soil stand for those who hear the message and retain
it in a good and obedient heart, and they persist
until they bear fruit.

A Lamp under a Bowl
(Mark 4.21–25)

16 "No one lights a lamp and covers it with a
bowl or puts it under a bed. Instead, he puts it on
the lampstand, so that people will see the light as
they come in.

17 "Whatever is hidden away will be brought out

into the open, and whatever is covered up will be found and brought to light.

18 "Be careful, then, how you listen; because whoever has something will be given more, but whoever has nothing will have taken away from him even the little he thinks he has."

Jesus' Mother and Brothers
(Matt. 12.46-50; Mark 3.31-35)

19 Jesus' mother and brothers came to him, but were unable to join him because of the crowd. 20 Someone said to Jesus, "Your mother and brothers are standing outside and want to see you."

21 Jesus said to them all, "My mother and brothers are those who hear the word of God and obey it."

Jesus Calms a Storm
(Matt. 8.23-27; Mark 4.35-41)

22 One day Jesus got into a boat with his disciples and said to them, "Let us go across to the other side of the lake." So they started out. 23 As they were sailing, Jesus fell asleep. Suddenly a strong wind blew down on the lake, and the boat began to fill with water, so that they were all in great danger. 24 The disciples went to Jesus and woke him up, saying, "Master, Master! We are about to die!"

Jesus got up and gave an order to the wind and the stormy water; they died down, and there was a great calm. 25 Then he said to the disciples, "Where is your faith?"

But they were amazed and afraid, and said to one another, "Who is this man? He gives orders to the winds and waves, and they obey him!"

Jesus Heals a Man with Demons
(Matt. 8.28-34; Mark 5.1-20)

26 Jesus and his disciples sailed on over to the territory of Gerasa,g which is across the lake from Galilee. 27 As Jesus stepped ashore, he was met by a man from the town who had demons in him. For

gGerasa; some manuscripts have Gadara (see Mt 8.28); others have Gergesa.

a long time this man had gone without clothes and would not stay at home, but spent his time in the burial caves. 28When he saw Jesus, he gave a loud cry, threw himself down at his feet, and shouted, "Jesus, Son of the Most High God! What do you want with me? I beg you, don't punish me!" 29He said this because Jesus had ordered the evil spirit to go out of him. Many times it had seized him, and even though he was kept a prisoner, his hands and feet fastened with chains, he would break the chains and be driven by the demon out into the desert.

30 Jesus asked him, "What is your name?"

"My name is 'Mob,' " he answered—because many demons had gone into him. 31The demons begged Jesus not to send them into the abyss.h

32 There was a large herd of pigs near by, feeding on a hillside. So the demons begged Jesus to let them go into the pigs, and he let them. 33They went out of the man and into the pigs. The whole herd rushed down the side of the cliff into the lake and was drowned.

34 The men who had been taking care of the pigs saw what happened, so they ran off and spread the news in the town and among the farms. 35People went out to see what had happened, and when they came to Jesus, they found the man from whom the demons had gone out sitting at the feet of Jesus, clothed and in his right mind; and they were all afraid. 36Those who had seen it told the people how the man had been cured. 37Then all the people from that territory asked Jesus to go away, because they were terribly afraid. So Jesus got into the boat and left. 38The man from whom the demons had gone out begged Jesus, "Let me go with you."

But Jesus sent him away, saying, 39"Go back home and tell what God has done for you."

The man went through the town, telling what Jesus had done for him.

hABYSS: *It was thought that the demons were to be imprisoned in the depths of the earth until their final punishment.*

Jairus' Daughter and the Woman
Who Touched Jesus' Cloak
(Matt. 9.18–26; Mark 5.21–43)

40 When Jesus returned to the other side of the lake, the people welcomed him, because they had all been waiting for him. 41Then a man named Jairus arrived; he was an official in the local synagogue. He threw himself down at Jesus' feet and begged him to go to his home, 42because his only daughter, who was twelve years old, was dying.

As Jesus went along, the people were crowding him from every side. 43Among them was a woman who had suffered from severe bleeding for twelve years; she had spent all she had on doctors,*i* but no one had been able to cure her. 44She came up in the crowd behind Jesus and touched the edge of his cloak, and her bleeding stopped at once. 45Jesus asked, "Who touched me?"

Everyone denied it, and Peter said, "Master, the people are all round you and crowding in on you."

46 But Jesus said, "Someone touched me, for I knew it when power went out of me." 47The woman saw that she had been found out, so she came trembling and threw herself at Jesus' feet. There in front of everybody, she told him why she had touched him and how she had been healed at once. 48Jesus said to her, "My daughter, your faith has made you well. Go in peace."

49 While Jesus was saying this, a messenger came from the official's house. "Your daughter has died," he told Jairus; "don't bother the Teacher any longer."

50 But Jesus heard it and said to Jairus, "Don't be afraid; only believe, and she will be well."

51 When he arrived at the house, he would not let anyone go in with him except Peter, John, and James, and the child's father and mother. 52Everyone there was crying and mourning for the child. Jesus said, "Don't cry; the child is not dead—she is only sleeping!"

i Some manuscripts do not have she had spent all she had on doctors.

53 They all laughed at him, because they knew that she was dead. 54But Jesus took her by the hand and called out, "Get up, my child!" 55Her life returned, and she got up at once, and Jesus ordered them to give her something to eat. 56Her parents were astounded, but Jesus commanded them not to tell anyone what had happened.

Jesus Sends Out the Twelve Disciples
(Matt. 10.5–15; Mark 6.7–13)

9 Jesus called the twelve disciples together and gave them power and authority to drive out all demons and to cure diseases. 2Then he sent them out to preach the Kingdom of God and to heal the sick, 3after saying to them, "Take nothing with you for the journey: no stick, no beggar's bag, no food, no money, not even an extra shirt. 4Wherever you are welcomed, stay in the same house until you leave that town; 5wherever people don't welcome you, leave that town and shake the dust off your feet as a warning to them."

6 The disciples left and travelled through all the villages, preaching the Good News and healing people everywhere.

Herod's Confusion
(Matt. 14.1–12; Mark 6.14–29)

7 When Herod, the ruler of Galilee, heard about all the things that were happening, he was very confused, because some people were saying that John the Baptist had come back to life. 8Others were saying that Elijah had appeared, and still others that one of the prophets of long ago had come back to life. 9Herod said, "I had John's head cut off; but who is this man I hear these things about?" And he kept trying to see Jesus.

Jesus Feeds Five Thousand Men
(Matt. 14.13–21; Mark 6.30–44; John 6.1–14)

10 The apostles came back and told Jesus everything they had done. He took them with him, and they went off by themselves to a town called Bethsaida. 11When the crowds heard about it, they followed him.

He welcomed them, spoke to them about the Kingdom of God, and healed those who needed it.

12 When the sun was beginning to set, the twelve disciples came to him and said, "Send the people away so that they can go to the villages and farms round here and find food and lodging, because this is a lonely place."

13 But Jesus said to them, "You yourselves give them something to eat."

They answered, "All we have are five loaves and two fish. Do you want us to go and buy food for this whole crowd?" 14(There were about five thousand men there.)

Jesus said to his disciples, "Make the people sit down in groups of about fifty each."

15 After the disciples had done so, 16 Jesus took the five loaves and two fish, looked up to heaven, thanked God for them, broke them, and gave them to the disciples to distribute to the people. 17 They all

They all ate and had enough (9.17)

ate and had enough, and the disciples took up twelve baskets of what was left over.

Peter's Declaration about Jesus
(Matt. 16.13–19; Mark 8.27–29)

18 One day when Jesus was praying alone, the disciples came to him. "Who do the crowds say I am?" he asked them.

19 "Some say that you are John the Baptist," they answered. "Others say that you are Elijah, while others say that one of the prophets of long ago has come back to life."

20 "What about you?" he asked them. "Who do you say I am?"

Peter answered, "You are God's Messiah."

Jesus Speaks about His Suffering and Death
(Matt. 16.20–28; Mark 8.30—9.1)

21 Then Jesus gave them strict orders not to tell this to anyone. 22 He also said to them, "The Son of Man must suffer much and be rejected by the elders, the chief priests, and the teachers of the Law. He will be put to death, but three days later he will be raised to life."

23 And he said to them all, "If anyone wants to come with me, he must forget self, take up his cross every day, and follow me. 24 For whoever wants to save his own life will lose it, but whoever loses his life for my sake will save it. 25 Will a person gain anything if he wins the whole world but is himself lost or defeated? Of course not! 26 If a person is ashamed of me and of my teaching, then the Son of Man will be ashamed of him when he comes in his glory and in the glory of the Father and of the holy angels. 27 I assure you that there are some here who will not die until they have seen the Kingdom of God."

The Transfiguration
(Matt. 17.1–8; Mark 9.2–8)

28 About a week after he had said these things, Jesus took Peter, John, and James with him and went up a hill to pray. 29 While he was praying, his face

changed its appearance, and his clothes became dazzling white. 30 Suddenly two men were there talking with him. They were Moses and Elijah, 31 who appeared in heavenly glory and talked with Jesus about the way in which he would soon fulfil God's purpose by dying in Jerusalem. 32 Peter and his companions were sound asleep, but they woke up and saw Jesus' glory and the two men who were standing with him. 33 As the men were leaving Jesus, Peter said to him, "Master, how good it is that we are here! We will make three tents, one for you, one for Moses, and one for Elijah." (He did not really know what he was saying.)

34 While he was still speaking, a cloud appeared and covered them with its shadow; and the disciples were afraid as the cloud came over them. 35 A voice said from the cloud, "This is my Son, whom I have chosen—listen to him!"

36 When the voice stopped, there was Jesus all alone. The disciples kept quiet about all this, and told no one at that time anything they had seen.

Jesus Heals a Boy with an Evil Spirit
(Matt. 17.14–18; Mark 9.14–27)

37 The next day Jesus and the three disciples went down from the hill, and a large crowd met Jesus. 38 A man shouted from the crowd, "Teacher! I beg you, look at my son—my only son! 39 A spirit attacks him with a sudden shout and throws him into a fit, so that he foams at the mouth; it keeps on hurting him and will hardly let him go! 40 I begged your disciples to drive it out, but they couldn't."

41 Jesus answered, "How unbelieving and wrong you people are! How long must I stay with you? How long do I have to put up with you?" Then he said to the man, "Bring your son here."

42 As the boy was coming, the demon knocked him to the ground and threw him into a fit. Jesus gave a command to the evil spirit, healed the boy, and gave him back to his father. 43 All the people were amazed at the mighty power of God.

Jesus Speaks Again about His Death
(Matt. 17.22-23; Mark 9.30-32)

The people were still marvelling at everything Jesus was doing, when he said to his disciples, 44"Don't forget what I am about to tell you! The Son of Man is going to be handed over to the power of men." 45But the disciples did not know what this meant. It had been hidden from them so that they could not understand it, and they were afraid to ask him about the matter.

Who Is the Greatest?
(Matt. 18.1-5; Mark 9.33-37)

46 An argument broke out among the disciples as to which one of them was the greatest. 47 Jesus knew what they were thinking, so he took a child, stood him by his side, 48 and said to them, "Whoever welcomes this child in my name, welcomes me; and whoever welcomes me, also welcomes the one who sent me. For he who is least among you all is the greatest."

Whoever Is Not against You Is for You
(Mark 9.38-40)

49 John spoke up, "Master, we saw a man driving out demons in your name, and we told him to stop, because he doesn't belong to our group."

50 "Do not try to stop him," Jesus said to him and to the other disciples, "because whoever is not against you is for you."

A Samaritan Village Refuses to Receive Jesus

51 As the time drew near when Jesus would be taken up to heaven, he made up his mind and set out on his way to Jerusalem. 52 He sent messengers ahead of him, who went into a village in Samaria to get everything ready for him. 53 But the people there would not receive him, because it was clear that he was on his way to Jerusalem. 54 When the disciples James and John saw this, they said, "Lord,

do you want us to call fire down from heaven to destroy them?"*j*

55 Jesus turned and rebuked them.*k* 56Then Jesus and his disciples went on to another village.

The Would-be Followers of Jesus
(Matt. 8.19–22)

57 As they went on their way, a man said to Jesus, "I will follow you wherever you go."

58 Jesus said to him, "Foxes have holes, and birds have nests, but the Son of Man has nowhere to lie down and rest."

59 He said to another man, "Follow me."

But that man said, "Sir, first let me go back and bury my father."

60 Jesus answered, "Let the dead bury their own dead. You go and proclaim the Kingdom of God."

61 Another man said, "I will follow you, sir; but first let me go and say good-bye to my family."

62 Jesus said to him, "Anyone who starts to plough and then keeps looking back is of no use to the Kingdom of God."

Jesus Sends Out the Seventy-two

10 After this the Lord chose another seventy-two*l* men and sent them out two by two, to go ahead of him to every town and place where he himself was about to go. 2He said to them, "There is a large harvest, but few workers to gather it in. Pray to the owner of the harvest that he will send out workers to gather in his harvest. 3Go! I am sending you like lambs among wolves. 4Don't take a purse or a beggar's bag or shoes; don't stop to greet anyone on the road. 5Whenever you go into a house, first say, 'Peace be with this house.' 6If a peace-loving man lives there, let your greeting of peace remain on him; if not, take back your greeting of peace. 7Stay in that same house, eating and drinking whatever

j Some manuscripts add as Elijah did.
k Some manuscripts add and said, "You don't know what kind of a Spirit you belong to; for the Son of Man did not come to destroy men's lives, but to save them."
*l*seventy-two; *some manuscripts have* seventy.

they offer you, for a worker should be given his pay.
Don't move round from one house to another. 8 Whenever you go into a town and are made welcome,
eat what is set before you, 9 heal the sick in that
town, and say to the people there, 'The Kingdom
of God has come near you.' 10 But whenever you go
into a town and are not welcomed, go out in the
streets and say, 11 'Even the dust from your town
that sticks to our feet we wipe off against you. But
remember that the Kingdom of God has come near
you!' 12 I assure you that on Judgement Day God
will show more mercy to Sodom than to that town!

The Unbelieving Towns
(Matt. 11.20–24)

13 "How terrible it will be for you, Chorazin! How
terrible for you too, Bethsaida! If the miracles which
were performed in you had been performed in Tyre
and Sidon, the people there would long ago have
sat down, put on sackcloth, and sprinkled ashes on
themselves, to show that they had turned from their
sins! 14 God will show more mercy on Judgement Day
to Tyre and Sidon than to you. 15 And as for you,
Capernaum! Did you want to lift yourself up to
heaven? You will be thrown down to hell!"

16 Jesus said to his disciples, "Whoever listens to
you listens to me; whoever rejects you rejects me;
and whoever rejects me rejects the one who sent
me."

The Return of the Seventy-two

17 The seventy-two[m] men came back in great joy.
"Lord," they said, "even the demons obeyed us when
we gave them a command in your name!"

18 Jesus answered them, "I saw Satan fall like
lightning from heaven. 19 Listen! I have given you
authority, so that you can walk on snakes and scorpions and overcome all the power of the Enemy, and
nothing will hurt you. 20 But don't be glad because
the evil spirits obey you; rather be glad because your
names are written in heaven."

[m] seventy-two; *some manuscripts have* seventy *(see verse 1).*

Jesus Rejoices
(Matt. 11.25–27; 13.16–17)

21 At that time Jesus was filled with joy by the Holy Spirit*n* and said, "Father, Lord of heaven and earth! I thank you because you have shown to the unlearned what you have hidden from the wise and learned. Yes, Father, this was how you wanted it to happen.

22 "My Father has given me all things. No one knows who the Son is except the Father, and no one knows who the Father is except the Son and those to whom the Son chooses to reveal him."

23 Then Jesus turned to the disciples and said to them privately, "How fortunate you are to see the things you see! 24 I tell you that many prophets and kings wanted to see what you see, but they could not, and to hear what you hear, but they did not."

The Parable of the Good Samaritan

25 A teacher of the Law came up and tried to trap Jesus. "Teacher," he asked, "what must I do to receive eternal life?"

26 Jesus answered him, "What do the Scriptures say? How do you interpret them?"

27 The man answered, " 'Love the Lord your God with all your heart, with all your soul, with all your strength, and with all your mind'; and 'Love your neighbour as you love yourself.' "

28 "You are right," Jesus replied; "do this and you will live."

29 But the teacher of the Law wanted to justify himself, so he asked Jesus, "Who is my neighbour?"

30 Jesus answered, "There was once a man who was going down from Jerusalem to Jericho when robbers attacked him, stripped him, and beat him up, leaving him half dead. 31 It so happened that a priest was going down that road; but when he saw the man, he walked on by, on the other side. 32 In the same way a Levite also came along, went over and

*n*by the Holy Spirit; *some manuscripts have* by the Spirit; *others have* in his spirit.

looked at the man, and then walked on by, on the other side. ³³But a Samaritan who was travelling that

His heart was filled with pity (10.33)

way came upon the man, and when he saw him, his heart was filled with pity. ³⁴He went over to him, poured oil and wine on his wounds and bandaged them; then he put the man on his own animal and took him to an inn, where he took care of him. ³⁵The next day he took out two silver coins and gave them to the innkeeper. 'Take care of him,' he told the innkeeper, 'and when I come back this way, I will pay you whatever else you spend on him.' "

36 And Jesus concluded, "In your opinion, which one of these three acted like a neighbour towards the man attacked by the robbers?"

37 The teacher of the Law answered, "The one who was kind to him."

Jesus replied, "You go, then, and do the same."

Jesus Visits Martha and Mary

38 As Jesus and his disciples went on their way, he came to a village where a woman named Martha welcomed him in her home. ³⁹She had a sister named

Mary, who sat down at the feet of the Lord and listened to his teaching. ⁴⁰Martha was upset over all the work she had to do, so she came and said, "Lord, don't you care that my sister has left me to do all the work by myself? Tell her to come and help me!"

41 The Lord answered her, "Martha, Martha! You are worried and troubled over so many things, ⁴²but just one is needed. Mary has chosen the right thing, and it will not be taken away from her."

Jesus' Teaching on Prayer
(Matt. 6.9–13; 7.7–11)

11 One day Jesus was praying in a certain place. When he had finished, one of his disciples said to him, "Lord, teach us to pray, just as John taught his disciples."

2 Jesus said to them, "When you pray, say this:
'Father:
    May your holy name be honoured;
    may your Kingdom come.
3   Give us day by day the food we need.ᵒ
4   Forgive us our sins,
    for we forgive everyone who does us wrong.
    And do not bring us to hard testing.' "

5 And Jesus said to his disciples, "Suppose one of you should go to a friend's house at midnight and say to him, 'Friend, let me borrow three loaves of bread. ⁶A friend of mine who is on a journey has just come to my house, and I haven't got any food for him!' ⁷And suppose your friend should answer from inside, 'Don't bother me! The door is already locked, and my children and I are in bed. I can't get up and give you anything.' ⁸Well, what then? I tell you that even if he will not get up and give you the bread because you are his friend, yet he will get up and give you everything you need because you are not ashamed to keep on asking.

9 "And so I say to you: Ask, and you will receive; seek, and you will find; knock, and the door will be opened to you. ¹⁰For everyone who asks will receive, and he who seeks will find, and the door will be opened

ᵒthe food we need; or food for the next day.

to anyone who knocks. ¹¹Would any of you who are fathers give your son a snake when he asks for fish? ¹²Or would you give him a scorpion when he asks for an egg? ¹³Bad as you are, you know how to give good things to your children. How much more, then, will the Father in heaven give the Holy Spirit to those who ask him!"

Jesus and Beelzebul
(Matt. 12.22-30; Mark 3.20-27)

14 Jesus was driving out a demon that could not talk; and when the demon went out, the man began to talk. The crowds were amazed, ¹⁵but some of the people said, "It is Beelzebul, the chief of the demons, who gives him the power to drive them out."

16 Others wanted to trap Jesus, so they asked him to perform a miracle to show that God approved of him. ¹⁷But Jesus knew what they were thinking, so he said to them, "Any country that divides itself into groups which fight each other will not last very long; a family divided against itself falls apart. ¹⁸So if Satan's kingdom has groups fighting each other, how can it last? You say that I drive out demons because Beelzebul gives me the power to do so. ¹⁹If this is how I drive them out, how do your followers drive them out? Your own followers prove that you are wrong! ²⁰No, it is rather by means of God's power that I drive out demons, and this proves that the Kingdom of God has already come to you.

21 "When a strong man, with all his weapons ready, guards his own house, all his belongings are safe. ²²But when a stronger man attacks him and defeats him, he carries away all the weapons the owner was depending on and divides up what he stole.

23 "Anyone who is not for me is really against me; anyone who does not help me gather is really scattering.

The Return of the Evil Spirit
(Matt. 12.43-45)

24 "When an evil spirit goes out of a person, it travels over dry country looking for a place to rest. If it can't find one, it says to itself, 'I will go back

to my house.' 25 So it goes back and finds the house clean and tidy. 26 Then it goes out and brings seven other spirits even worse than itself, and they come and live there. So when it is all over, that person is in a worse state than he was at the beginning."

True Happiness

27 When Jesus had said this, a woman spoke up from the crowd and said to him, "How happy is the woman who bore you and nursed you!"

28 But Jesus answered, "Rather, how happy are those who hear the word of God and obey it!"

The Demand for a Miracle
(Matt. 12.38–42)

29 As the people crowded round Jesus, he went on to say, "How evil are the people of this day! They ask for a miracle, but none will be given them except the miracle of Jonah. 30 In the same way that the prophet Jonah was a sign for the people of Nineveh, so the Son of Man will be a sign for the people of this day. 31 On Judgement Day the Queen of Sheba will stand up and accuse the people of today, because she travelled all the way from her country to listen to King Solomon's wise teaching; and I tell you there is something here greater than Solomon. 32 On Judgement Day the people of Nineveh will stand up and accuse you, because they turned from their sins when they heard Jonah preach; and I assure you that there is something here greater than Jonah!

The Light of the Body
(Matt. 5.15; 6.22–23)

33 "No one lights a lamp and then hides it or puts it under a bowl;*p* instead, he puts it on the lampstand, so that people may see the light as they come in. 34 Your eyes are like a lamp for the body. When your eyes are sound, your whole body is full of light; but when your eyes are no good, your whole body will be in darkness. 35 Make certain, then, that the light in you is not darkness. 36 If your whole body is

p Some manuscripts do not have or puts it under a bowl.

full of light, with no part of it in darkness, it will
be bright all over, as when a lamp shines on you
with its brightness."

Jesus Accuses the Pharisees and the Teachers of the Law
(Matt. 23.1–36; Mark 12.38–40)

37 When Jesus finished speaking, a Pharisee invited
him to eat with him; so he went in and sat down
to eat. 38 The Pharisee was surprised when he noticed
that Jesus had not washed before eating. 39 So the Lord
said to him, "Now then, you Pharisees clean the outside
of your cup and plate, but inside you are full of
violence and evil. 40 Fools! Did not God, who made
the outside, also make the inside? 41 But give what
is in your cups and plates to the poor, and everything
will be ritually clean for you.

42 "How terrible for you Pharisees! You give God
a tenth of the seasoning herbs, such as mint and
rue and all the other herbs, but you neglect justice
and love for God. These you should practise, without
neglecting the others.

43 "How terrible for you Pharisees! You love the
reserved seats in the synagogues and to be greeted
with respect in the market-places. 44 How terrible for
you! You are like unmarked graves which people walk
on without knowing it."

45 One of the teachers of the Law said to him,
"Teacher, when you say this, you insult us too!"

46 Jesus answered, "How terrible also for you
teachers of the Law! You put loads on people's backs
which are hard to carry, but you yourselves will not
stretch out a finger to help them carry those loads.
47 How terrible for you! You make fine tombs for
the prophets—the very prophets your ancestors murdered. 48 You yourselves admit, then, that you approve
of what your ancestors did; they murdered the prophets, and you build their tombs. 49 For this reason
the Wisdom of God said, 'I will send them prophets
and messengers; they will kill some of them and per-
secute others.' 50 So the people of this time will be
punished for the murder of all the prophets killed
since the creation of the world, 51 from the murder

of Abel to the murder of Zechariah, who was killed between the altar and the Holy Place. Yes, I tell you, the people of this time will be punished for them all!

52 "How terrible for you teachers of the Law! You have kept the key that opens the door to the house of knowledge; you yourselves will not go in, and you stop those who are trying to go in!"

53 When Jesus left that place, the teachers of the Law and the Pharisees began to criticize him bitterly and ask him questions about many things, 54trying to lay traps for him and catch him saying something wrong.

A Warning against Hypocrisy
(Matt. 10.26–27)

12 As thousands of people crowded together, so that they were stepping on each other, Jesus said first to his disciples, "Be on guard against the yeast of the Pharisees—I mean their hypocrisy. 2Whatever is covered up will be uncovered, and every secret will be made known. 3So then, whatever you have said in the dark will be heard in broad daylight, and whatever you have whispered in private in a closed room will be shouted from the housetops.

Whom to Fear
(Matt. 10.28–31)

4 "I tell you, my friends, do not be afraid of those who kill the body but cannot afterwards do anything worse. 5I will show you whom to fear: fear God, who, after killing, has the authority to throw into hell. Believe me, he is the one you must fear!

6 "Aren't five sparrows sold for two pennies? Yet not one sparrow is forgotten by God. 7Even the hairs of your head have all been counted. So do not be afraid; you are worth much more than many sparrows!

Confessing and Rejecting Christ
(Matt. 10.32–33; 12.32; 10.19–20)

8 "I assure you that whoever declares publicly that he belongs to me, the Son of Man will do the same for him before the angels of God. 9But whoever rejects

me publicly, the Son of Man will also reject him before the angels of God.

10 "Anyone who says a word against the Son of Man can be forgiven; but whoever says evil things against the Holy Spirit will not be forgiven.

11 "When they bring you to be tried in the synagogues or before governors or rulers, do not be worried about how you will defend yourself or what you will say. 12 For the Holy Spirit will teach you at that time what you should say."

The Parable of the Rich Fool

13 A man in the crowd said to Jesus, "Teacher, tell my brother to divide with me the property our father left us."

14 Jesus answered him, "My friend, who gave me the right to judge or to divide the property between you two?" 15 And he went on to say to them all, "Watch out and guard yourselves from every kind of greed; because a person's true life is not made up of the things he owns, no matter how rich he may be."

16 Then Jesus told them this parable: "There was once a rich man who had land which bore good crops. 17 He began to think to himself, 'I haven't anywhere to keep all my crops. What can I do? 18 This is what I will do,' he told himself; 'I will tear down my barns and build bigger ones, where I will store my corn and all my other goods. 19 Then I will say to myself, Lucky man! You have all the good things you need for many years. Take life easy, eat, drink, and enjoy yourself!' 20 But God said to him, 'You fool! This very night you will have to give up your life; then who will get all these things you have kept for yourself?' "

21 And Jesus concluded, "This is how it is with those who pile up riches for themselves but are not rich in God's sight."

Trust in God
(Matt. 6.25–34)

22 Then Jesus said to the disciples, "And so I tell you not to worry about the food you need to stay

And so I tell you not to worry (12.22)

alive or about the clothes you need for your body. 23 Life is much more important than food, and the body much more important than clothes. 24 Look at the crows: they don't sow seeds or gather a harvest; they don't have store-rooms or barns; God feeds them! You are worth so much more than birds! 25 Can any of you live a bit longer q by worrying about it? 26 If you can't manage even such a small thing, why worry about the other things? 27 Look how the wild flowers grow; they don't work or make clothes for themselves. But I tell you that not even King Solomon with all his wealth had clothes as beautiful as one of these flowers. 28 It is God who clothes the wild grass—grass that is here today and gone tomorrow, burnt up in the oven. Won't he be all the more sure to clothe you? How little faith you have!

29 "So don't be all upset, always concerned about what you will eat and drink. 30 (For the pagans of this world are always concerned about all these things.) Your Father knows that you need these things. 31 Instead, be concerned with his Kingdom, and he will provide you with these things.

Riches in Heaven
(Matt. 6.19–21)

32 "Do not be afraid, little flock, for your Father is pleased to give you the Kingdom. 33 Sell all your belongings and give the money to the poor. Provide for yourselves purses that don't wear out, and save

q live a bit longer; *or* grow a bit taller.

your riches in heaven, where they will never decrease, because no thief can get to them, and no moth can destroy them. 34 For your heart will always be where your riches are.

Watchful Servants

35 "Be ready for whatever comes, dressed for action and with your lamps lit, 36 like servants who are waiting for their master to come back from a wedding feast. When he comes and knocks, they will open the door for him at once. 37 How happy are those servants whose master finds them awake and ready when he returns! I tell you, he will take off his coat, ask them to sit down, and will wait on them. 38 How happy they are if he finds them ready, even if he should come at midnight or even later! 39 And you can be sure that if the owner of a house knew the time when the thief would come, he would not let the thief break into his house. 40 And you, too, must be ready, because the Son of Man will come at an hour when you are not expecting him."

The Faithful or the Unfaithful Servant
(Matt. 24.45-51)

41 Peter said, "Lord does this parable apply to us, or do you mean it for everyone?"

42 The Lord answered, "Who, then, is the faithful and wise servant? He is the one that his master will put in charge, to run the household and give the other servants their share of the food at the proper time. 43 How happy that servant is if his master finds him doing this when he comes home! 44 Indeed, I tell you, the master will put that servant in charge of all his property. 45 But if that servant says to himself that his master is taking a long time to come back and if he begins to beat the other servants, both the men and the women, and eats and drinks and gets drunk, 46 then the master will come back one day when the servant does not expect him and at a time he does not know. The master will cut him

in pieces^r and make him share the fate of the disobedient.

47 "The servant who knows what his master wants him to do, but does not get himself ready and do it, will be punished with a heavy whipping. 48But the servant who does not know what his master wants, and yet does something for which he deserves a whipping, will be punished with a light whipping. Much is required from the person to whom much is given; much more is required from the person to whom much more is given.

Jesus the Cause of Division
(Matt. 10.34–36)

49 "I came to set the earth on fire, and how I wish it were already kindled! 50I have a baptism to receive, and how distressed. I am until it is over! 51Do you suppose that I came to bring peace to the world? No, not peace, but division. 52From now on a family of five will be divided, three against two and two against three. 53Fathers will be against their sons, and sons against their fathers; mothers will be against their daughters, and daughters against their mothers; mothers-in-law will be against their daughters-in-law, and daughters-in-law against their mothers-in-law."

Understanding the Time
(Matt. 16.2–3)

54 Jesus said also to the people, "When you see a cloud coming up in the west, at once you say that it is going to rain—and it does. 55And when you feel the south wind blowing, you say that it is going to get hot—and it does. 56Hypocrites! You can look at the earth and the sky and predict the weather; why, then, don't you know the meaning of this present time?

Settle with Your Opponent
(Matt. 5.25–26)

57 "Why do you not judge for yourselves the right thing to do? 58If someone brings a lawsuit against you and takes you to court, do your best to settle

^rcut him in pieces; *or* throw him out.

the dispute with him before you get to court. If you
don't, he will drag you before the judge, who will
hand you over to the police, and you will be put
in jail. ⁵⁹There you will stay, I tell you, until you
pay the last penny of your fine."

Turn from Your Sins or Die

13 At that time some people were there who told
Jesus about the Galileans whom Pilate had killed
while they were offering sacrifices to God. ²Jesus
answered them, "Because those Galileans were killed
in that way, do you think it proves that they were
worse sinners than all the other Galileans? ³No indeed!
And I tell you that if you do not turn from your
sins, you will all die as they did. ⁴What about those
eighteen people in Siloam who were killed when the
tower fell on them? Do you suppose this proves that
they were worse than all the other people living in
Jerusalem? ⁵No indeed! And I tell you that if you
do not turn from your sins, you will all die as they
did."

The Parable of the Unfruitful Fig-Tree

6 Then Jesus told them this parable: "There was
once a man who had a fig-tree growing in his vineyard.
He went looking for figs on it but found none. ⁷So
he said to his gardener, 'Look, for three years I have
been coming here looking for figs on this fig-tree,
and I haven't found any. Cut it down! Why should
it go on using up the soil?' ⁸But the gardener answered,
'Leave it alone, sir, just one more year; I will dig
round it and put in some manure. ⁹Then if the tree
bears figs next year, so much the better; if not, then
you can have it cut down.' "

Jesus Heals a Crippled Woman on the Sabbath

10 One Sabbath Jesus was teaching in a synagogue.
¹¹A woman there had an evil spirit that had made
her ill for eighteen years; she was bent over and
could not straighten up at all. ¹²When Jesus saw
her, he called out to her, "Woman, you are free from
your illness!" ¹³He placed his hands on her, and at
once she straightened herself up and praised God.

14 The official of the synagogue was angry that Jesus had healed on the Sabbath, so he spoke up and said to the people, "There are six days in which we should work; so come during those days and be healed, but not on the Sabbath!"

15 The Lord answered him, "You hypocrites! Any one of you would untie his ox or his donkey from the stall and take it out to give it water on the Sabbath. 16 Now here is this descendant of Abraham whom Satan has kept bound up for eighteen years; should she not be released on the Sabbath?" 17 His answer made his enemies ashamed of themselves, while the people rejoiced over all the wonderful things that he did.

The Parable of the Mustard Seed
(Matt. 13.31-32; Mark 4.30-32)

18 Jesus asked, "What is the Kingdom of God like? What shall I compare it with? 19 It is like this. A man takes a mustard seed and sows it in his field. The plant grows and becomes a tree, and the birds make their nests in its branches."

The Parable of the Yeast
(Matt. 13.33)

20 Again Jesus asked, "What shall I compare the Kingdom of God with? 21 It is like this. A woman takes some yeast and mixes it with forty litres of flour until the whole batch of dough rises."

The Narrow Door
(Matt. 7.13-14, 21-23)

22 Jesus went through towns and villages, teaching the people and making his way towards Jerusalem. 23 Someone asked him, "Sir, will just a few people be saved?"

Jesus answered them, 24 "Do your best to go in through the narrow door; because many people will surely try to go in but will not be able. 25 The master of the house will get up and close the door; then when you stand outside and begin to knock on the door and say, 'Open the door for us, sir!' he will answer you, 'I don't know where you come from!'

²⁶Then you will answer, 'We ate and drank with you; you taught in our town!' ²⁷But he will say again, 'I don't know where you come from. Get away from me, all you wicked people!' ²⁸How you will cry and grind your teeth when you see Abraham, Isaac, and Jacob, and all the prophets in the Kingdom of God, while you are thrown out! ²⁹People will come from the east and the west, from the north and the south, and sit down at the feast in the Kingdom of God. ³⁰Then those who are now last will be first, and those who are now first will be last."

Jesus' Love for Jerusalem
(Matt. 23.37-39)

31 At that same time some Pharisees came to Jesus and said to him, "You must get out of here and go somewhere else, because Herod wants to kill you."

32 Jesus answered them, "Go and tell that fox: 'I am driving out demons and performing cures today and tomorrow, and on the third day I shall finish my work.' ³³Yet I must be on my way today, tomorrow, and the next day; it is not right for a prophet to be killed anywhere except in Jerusalem.

34 "Jerusalem, Jerusalem! You kill the prophets, you stone the messengers God has sent you! How many times have I wanted to put my arms round all your people, just as a hen gathers her chicks under her wings, but you would not let me! ³⁵And so your Temple will be abandoned. I assure you that you will not see me until the time comes when you say, 'God bless him who comes in the name of the Lord.' "

Jesus Heals a Sick Man

14 One Sabbath Jesus went to eat a meal at the home of one of the leading Pharisees; and people were watching Jesus closely. ²A man whose legs and arms were swollen came to Jesus, ³and Jesus asked the teachers of the Law and the Pharisees, "Does our Law allow healing on the Sabbath or not?"

4 But they would not say anything. Jesus took the man, healed him, and sent him away. ⁵Then he said to them, "If any one of you had a son or an ox—

that happened to fall in a well on a Sabbath, would you not pull him out at once on the Sabbath itself?"

6 But they were not able to answer him about this.

Humility and Hospitality

7 Jesus noticed how some of the guests were choosing the best places, so he told this parable to all of them: 8"When someone invites you to a wedding feast, do not sit down in the best place. It could happen that someone more important than you has been invited, 9and your host, who invited both of you, would have to come and say to you, 'Let him have this place.' Then you would be embarrassed and have to sit in the lowest place. 10Instead, when you are invited, go and sit in the lowest place, so that your host will come to you and say, 'Come on up, my friend, to a better place.' This will bring you honour in the presence of all the other guests. 11For everyone who makes himself great will be humbled, and everyone who humbles himself will be made great."

12 Then Jesus said to his host, "When you give a lunch or a dinner, do not invite your friends or your brothers or your relatives or your rich neighbours—for they will invite you back, and in this way you will be paid for what you did. 13When you give a feast, invite the poor, the crippled, the lame, and the blind; 14and you will be blessed, because they are not able to pay you back. God will repay you on the day the good people rise from death."

The Parable of the Great Feast
(Matt. 22.1–10)

15 When one of the men sitting at table heard this, he said to Jesus, "How happy are those who will sit down at the feast in the Kingdom of God!"

16 Jesus said to him, "There was once a man who was giving a great feast to which he invited many people. 17When it was time for the feast, he sent his servant to tell his guests, 'Come, everything is ready!' 18But they all began, one after another, to make excuses. The first one told the servant, 'I have bought a field and must go and look at it; please accept my apologies.' 19Another one said, 'I have

bought five pairs of oxen and am on my way to try them out; please accept my apologies.' 20 Another one said, 'I have just got married, and for that reason I cannot come.'

21 "The servant went back and told all this to his master. The master was furious and said to his servant, 'Hurry out to the streets and alleys of the town, and bring back the poor, the crippled, the blind, and the lame.' 22 Soon the servant said, 'Your order has been carried out, sir, but there is room for more.' 23 So the master said to the servant, 'Go out to the country roads and lanes and make people come in, so that my house will be full. 24 I tell you all that none of those men who were invited will taste my dinner!' "

The Cost of Being a Disciple
(Matt. 10.37–38)

25 Once when large crowds of people were going along with Jesus, he turned and said to them, 26 "Whoever comes to me cannot be my disciple unless he loves me more than he loves his father and his mother, his wife and his children, his brothers and his sisters, and himself as well. 27 Whoever does not carry his own cross and come after me cannot be my disciple.

28 "If one of you is planning to build a tower, he sits down first and works out what it will cost, to see if he has enough money to finish the job. 29 If he doesn't, he will not be able to finish the tower after laying the foundation; and all who see what happened will laugh at him. 30 'This man began to build but can't finish the job!' they will say.

31 "If a king goes out with ten thousand men to fight another king who comes against him with twenty thousand men, he will sit down first and decide if he is strong enough to face that other king. 32 If he isn't, he will send messengers to meet the other king, to ask for terms of peace while he is still a long way off. 33 In the same way," concluded Jesus, "none of you can be my disciple unless he gives up everything he has.

Worthless Salt
(Matt. 5.13; Mark 9.50)

34 "Salt is good, but if it loses its saltiness, there is no way to make it salty again. 35 It is no good for the soil or for the manure heap; it is thrown away. Listen, then, if you have ears!"

The Lost Sheep
(Matt. 18.12–14)

15 One day when many tax collectors and other outcasts came to listen to Jesus, 2 the Pharisees and the teachers of the Law started grumbling, "This man welcomes outcasts and even eats with them!" 3 So Jesus told them this parable:

4 "Suppose one of you has a hundred sheep and loses one of them—what does he do? He leaves the other ninety-nine sheep in the pasture and goes looking for the one that got lost until he finds it. 5 When he finds it, he is so happy that he puts it on his shoulders 6 and carries it back home. Then he calls his friends and neighbours together and says to them, 'I am so happy I found my lost sheep. Let us celebrate!' 7 In the same way, I tell you, there will be more joy in heaven over one sinner who repents than over ninety-nine respectable people who do not need to repent.

The Lost Coin

8 "Or suppose a woman who has ten silver coins loses one of them—what does she do? She lights a lamp, sweeps her house, and looks carefully everywhere until she finds it. 9 When she finds it, she calls her friends and neighbours together, and says to them, 'I am so happy I found the coin I lost. Let us celebrate!' 10 In the same way, I tell you, the angels of God rejoice over one sinner who repents."

The Lost Son

11 Jesus went on to say, "There was once a man who had two sons. 12 The younger one said to him, 'Father, give me my share of the property now.' So the man divided his property between his two sons.

¹³After a few days the younger son sold his part of the property and left home with the money. He went to a country far away, where he wasted his money in reckless living. ¹⁴He spent everything he had. Then a severe famine spread over that country, and he was left without a thing. ¹⁵So he went to work for one of the citizens of that country, who sent him out to his farm to take care of the pigs. ¹⁶He wished he could fill himself with the bean pods the pigs ate, but no one gave him anything to eat. ¹⁷At

Here I am about to starve! (15.17)

last he came to his senses and said, 'All my father's hired workers have more than they can eat, and here I am about to starve! ¹⁸I will get up and go to my father and say, Father, I have sinned against God and against you. ¹⁹I am no longer fit to be called your son; treat me as one of your hired workers.' ²⁰So he got up and started back to his father.

"He was still a long way from home when his father saw him; his heart was filled with pity, and he ran, threw his arms round his son, and kissed him. ²¹'Father,' the son said, 'I have sinned against God and against you. I am no longer fit to be called your son.' ²²But the father called his servants. 'Hurry!' he said. 'Bring the best robe and put it on him. Put a ring on his finger and shoes on his feet. ²³Then go and get the prize calf and kill it, and let us celebrate with a feast! ²⁴For this son of mine was dead, but now he is alive; he was lost, but now he has been found.' And so the feasting began.

25 "In the meantime the elder son was out in the

field. On his way back, when he came close to the house, he heard the music and dancing. 26 So he called one of the servants and asked him, 'What's going on?' 27 'Your brother has come back home,' the servant answered, 'and your father has killed the prize calf, because he got him back safe and sound.'

28 The elder brother was so angry that he would not go into the house; so his father came out and begged him to come in. 29 But he answered his father, 'Look, all these years I have worked for you like a slave, and I have never disobeyed your orders. What have you given me? Not even a goat for me to have a feast with my friends! 30 But this son of yours wasted all your property on prostitutes, and when he comes back home, you kill the prize calf for him!' 31 'My son,' the father answered, 'you are always here with me, and everything I have is yours. 32 But we

But now he is alive (15.32)

had to celebrate and be happy, because your brother was dead, but now he is alive; he was lost, but now he has been found.' "

The Shrewd Manager

16 Jesus said to his disciples, "There was once a rich man who had a servant who managed his property. The rich man was told that the manager was wasting his master's money, 2 so he called him in and said, 'What is this I hear about you? Hand in a complete account of your handling of my property, because you cannot be my manager any longer.' 3 The servant said to himself, 'My Master is going to dismiss me from my job. What shall I do? I am not strong enough to dig ditches, and I am ashamed to beg. 4 Now I know what I will do! Then when my job is gone, I shall have friends who will welcome me in their homes.'

5 "So he called in all the people who were in debt to his master. He asked the first one, 'How much do you owe my master?' 6 'One hundred barrels of olive-oil,' he answered. 'Here is your account,' the manager told him; 'sit down and write fifty.' 7 Then he asked another one, 'And you—how much do you owe?' 'A thousand sacks of wheat,' he answered. 'Here is your account,' the manager told him; 'write eight hundred.'

8 "As a result the master of this dishonest manager praised him for doing such a shrewd thing; because the people of this world are much more shrewd in handling their affairs than the people who belong to the light."

9 And Jesus went on to say, "And so I tell you: make friends for yourselves with worldly wealth, so that when it gives out, you will be welcomed in the eternal home. 10 Whoever is faithful in small matters will be faithful in large ones; whoever is dishonest in small matters will be dishonest in large ones. 11 If, then, you have not been faithful in handling worldly wealth, how can you be trusted with true wealth? 12 And if you have not been faithful with what belongs to someone else, who will give you what belongs to you?

13 "No servant can be the slave of two masters; he will hate one and love the other; he will be loyal to one and despise the other. You cannot serve both God and money."

Some Sayings of Jesus
(Matt. 11.12–13; 5.31–32; Mark 10.11–12)

14 When the Pharisees heard all this, they sneered at Jesus, because they loved money. 15 Jesus said to them, "You are the ones who make yourselves look right in other people's sight, but God knows your hearts. For the things that are considered of great value by man are worth nothing in God's sight.

16 "The Law of Moses and the writings of the prophets were in effect up to the time of John the Baptist; since then the Good News about the Kingdom of God is being told, and everyone forces his way in. 17 But it is easier for heaven and earth to disappear than for the smallest detail of the Law to be done away with.

18 "Any man who divorces his wife and marries another woman commits adultery; and the man who marries a divorced woman commits adultery.

The Rich Man and Lazarus

19 "There was once a rich man who dressed in the most expensive clothes and lived in great luxury every day. 20 There was also a poor man named Lazarus, covered with sores, who used to be brought to the rich man's door, 21 hoping to eat the bits of food that fell from the rich man's table. Even the dogs would come and lick his sores.

22 "The poor man died and was carried by the angels to sit beside Abraham at the feast in heaven. The rich man died and was buried, 23 and in Hades,^{s} where he was in great pain, he looked up and saw Abraham, far away, with Lazarus at his side. 24 So he called out, 'Father Abraham! Take pity on me, and send Lazarus to dip his finger in some water and cool my tongue, because I am in great pain in this fire!'

25 "But Abraham said, 'Remember, my son, that in your lifetime you were given all the good things, while Lazarus got all the bad things. But now he is enjoying himself here, while you are in pain. 26 Be-

^{s} HADES: *The world of the dead.*

sides all that, there is a deep pit lying between us, so that those who want to cross over from here to you cannot do so, nor can anyone cross over to us from where you are.' 27The rich man said, 'Then I beg you, father Abraham, send Lazarus to my father's house, 28where I have five brothers. Let him go and warn them so that they, at least, will not come to this place of pain.'

29 "Abraham said, 'Your brothers have Moses and the prophets to warn them; your brothers should listen to what they say.' 30The rich man answered, 'That is not enough, father Abraham! But if someone were to rise from death and go to them, then they would turn from their sins.' 31But Abraham said, 'If they will not listen to Moses and the prophets, they will not be convinced even if someone were to rise from death.' "

Sin
(Matt. 18.6–7, 21–22; Mark 9.42)

17 Jesus said to his disciples, "Things that make people fall into sin are bound to happen, but how terrible for the one who makes them happen! 2It would be better for him if a large millstone were tied round his neck and he were thrown into the sea than for him to cause one of these little ones to sin. 3So watch what you do!

"If your brother sins, rebuke him, and if he repents, forgive him. 4If he sins against you seven times in one day, and each time he comes to you saying, 'I repent,' you must forgive him."

Faith

5 The apostles said to the Lord, "Make our faith greater."

6 The Lord answered, "If you had faith as big as a mustard seed, you could say to this mulberry tree, 'Pull yourself up by the roots and plant yourself in the sea!' and it would obey you.

A Servant's Duty

7 "Suppose one of you has a servant who is ploughing or looking after the sheep. When he comes in

from the field, do you tell him to hurry and eat his meal? 8 Of course not! Instead, you say to him, 'Get my supper ready, then put on your apron and wait on me while I eat and drink; after that you may have your meal.' 9 The servant does not deserve thanks for obeying orders, does he? 10 It is the same with you; when you have done all you have been told to do, say, 'We are ordinary servants; we have only done our duty.' "

Jesus Heals Ten Men

11 As Jesus made his way to Jerusalem, he went along the border between Samaria and Galilee. 12 He was going into a village when he was met by ten men suffering from a dreaded skin-disease. They stood at a distance 13 and shouted, "Jesus! Master! Take pity on us!"

14 Jesus saw them and said to them, "Go and let the priests examine you."

On the way they were made clean.t 15 When one of them saw that he was healed, he came back, praising God in a loud voice. 16 He threw himself to the ground at Jesus' feet and thanked him. The man was a Samaritan. 17 Jesus said, "There were ten men who were healed; where are the other nine? 18 Why is this foreigner the only one who came back to give thanks to God?" 19 And Jesus said to him, "Get up and go; your faith has made you well."

The Coming of the Kingdom
(Matt. 24.23–28, 37–41)

20 Some Pharisees asked Jesus when the Kingdom of God would come. His answer was, "The Kingdom of God does not come in such a way as to be seen. 21 No one will say, 'Look, here it is!' or, 'There it is!'; because the Kingdom of God is within you."u

22 Then he said to the disciples, "The time will come when you will wish you could see one of the days of the Son of Man, but you will not see it. 23 There will be those who will say to you, 'Look,

t MADE CLEAN: *See 5.12.*
u within you; *or* among you, *or* will suddenly appear among you.

Where are the other nine? (17.17)

over there!' or, 'Look, over here!' But don't go out looking for it. 24 As the lightning flashes across the sky and lights it up from one side to the other, so will the Son of Man be in his day. 25 But first he must suffer much and be rejected by the people of this day. 26 As it was in the time of Noah so shall it be in the days of the Son of Man. 27 Everybody kept on eating and drinking, and men and women married, up to the very day Noah went into the boat and the flood came and killed them all. 28 It will be as it was in the time of Lot. Everybody kept on eating and drinking, buying and selling, planting and building. 29 On the day Lot left Sodom, fire and sulphur rained down from heaven and killed them all. 30 That is how it will be on the day the Son of Man is revealed.

31 "On that day the man who is on the roof of his house must not go down into the house to get his belongings; in the same way the man who is out in the field must not go back to the house. 32Remember Lot's wife! 33Whoever tries to save his own life will lose it; whoever loses his life will save it. 34On that night, I tell you, there will be two people sleeping in the same bed: one will be taken away, the other will be left behind. 35Two women will be grinding corn together: one will be taken away, the other will be left behind." *v*

37 The disciples asked him, "Where, Lord?"

Jesus answered, "Wherever there is a dead body, the vultures will gather."

The Parable of the Widow and the Judge

18 Then Jesus told his disciples a parable to teach them that they should always pray and never become discouraged. 2"In a certain town there was a judge who neither feared God nor respected man. 3And there was a widow in that same town who kept coming to him and pleading for her rights, saying, 'Help me against my opponent!' 4For a long time the judge refused to act, but at last he said to himself, 'Even though I don't fear God or respect man, 5yet because of all the trouble this widow is giving me, I will see to it that she gets her rights. If I don't, she will keep on coming and finally wear me out!' "

6 And the Lord continued, "Listen to what that corrupt judge said. 7Now, will God not judge in favour of his own people who cry to him day and night for help? Will he be slow to help them? 8I tell you, he will judge in their favour and do it quickly. But will the Son of Man find faith on earth when he comes?"

The Parable of the Pharisee and the Tax Collector

9 Jesus also told this parable to people who were sure of their own goodness and despised everybody

v Some manuscripts add verse 36: Two men will be working in a field: one will be taken away, the other will be left behind (see Mt 24.40).

else. 10"Once there were two men who went up to the Temple to pray: one was a Pharisee, the other a tax collector.

11 "The Pharisee stood apart by himself and prayed, w 'I thank you, God, that I am not greedy, dishonest, or an adulterer, like everybody else. I thank you that I am not like that tax collector over there. 12I fast two days a week, and I give you a tenth of all my income.'

13 "But the tax collector stood at a distance and would not even raise his face to heaven, but beat on his breast and said, 'God, have pity on me, a sinner!' 14I tell you," said Jesus, "the tax collector, and not the Pharisee, was in the right with God when he went home. For everyone who makes himself great will be humbled, and everyone who humbles himself will be made great."

Jesus Blesses Little Children
(Matt. 19.13–15; Mark 10.13–16)

15 Some people brought their babies to Jesus for him to place his hands on them. The disciples saw them and scolded them for doing so, 16but Jesus called the children to him and said, "Let the children come to me and do not stop them, because the Kingdom of God belongs to such as these. 17Remember this! Whoever does not receive the Kingdom of God like a child will never enter it."

The Rich Man
(Matt. 19.16–30; Mark 10.17–31)

18 A Jewish leader asked Jesus, "Good Teacher, what must I do to receive eternal life?"

19 "Why do you call me good?" Jesus asked him. "No one is good except God alone. 20You know the commandments: 'Do not commit adultery; do not commit murder; do not steal; do not accuse anyone falsely; respect your father and your mother.'"

21 The man replied, "Ever since I was young, I have obeyed all these commandments."

---

wstood apart by himself and prayed; *some manuscripts have* stood up and prayed to himself.

22 When Jesus heard this, he said to him, "There is still one more thing you need to do. Sell all you have and give the money to the poor, and you will have riches in heaven; then come and follow me." 23 But when the man heard this, he became very sad, because he was very rich.

24 Jesus saw that he was sad and said, "How hard it is for rich people to enter the Kingdom of God! 25 It is much harder for a rich person to enter the Kingdom of God than for a camel to go through the eye of a needle."

26 The people who heard him asked, "Who, then, can be saved?"

27 Jesus answered, "What is impossible for man is possible for God."

28 Then Peter said, "Look! We have left our homes to follow you."

29 "Yes," Jesus said to them, "and I assure you that anyone who leaves home or wife or brothers or parents or children for the sake of the Kingdom of God 30 will receive much more in this present age and eternal life in the age to come."

Jesus Speaks a Third Time about His Death
(Matt. 20.17–19; Mark 10.32–34)

31 Jesus took the twelve disciples aside and said to them, "Listen! We are going to Jerusalem where everything the prophets wrote about the Son of Man will come true. 32 He will be handed over to the Gentiles, who will mock him, insult him, and spit on him. 33 They will whip him and kill him, but three days later he will rise to life."

34 But the disciples did not understand any of these things; the meaning of the words was hidden from them, and they did not know what Jesus was talking about.

Jesus Heals a Blind Beggar
(Matt. 20.29–34; Mark 10.46–52)

35 As Jesus was coming near Jericho, there was a blind man sitting by the road, begging. 36 When he heard the crowd passing by, he asked, "What is this?"

37 "Jesus of Nazareth is passing by," they told him.

38 He cried out, "Jesus! Son of David! Take pity on me!"

39 The people in front scolded him and told him to be quiet. But he shouted even more loudly, "Son of David! Take pity on me!"

40 So Jesus stopped and ordered the blind man to be brought to him. When he came near, Jesus asked him, 41 "What do you want me to do for you?"

"Sir," he answered, "I want to see again."

42 Jesus said to him, "Then see! Your faith has made you well."

43 At once he was able to see, and he followed Jesus, giving thanks to God. When the crowd saw it, they all praised God.

Jesus and Zacchaeus

19 Jesus went on into Jericho and was passing through. 2 There was a chief tax collector there named Zacchaeus, who was rich. 3 He was trying to see who Jesus was, but he was a little man and could not see Jesus because of the crowd. 4 So he ran ahead of the crowd and climbed a sycomore tree to see Jesus, who was going to pass that way. 5 When Jesus came to that place, he looked up and said to Zacchaeus, "Hurry down, Zacchaeus, because I must stay in your house today."

6 Zacchaeus hurried down and welcomed him with great joy. 7 All the people who saw it started grumbling, "This man has gone as a guest to the home of a sinner!"

8 Zacchaeus stood up and said to the Lord, "Listen, sir! I will give half my belongings to the poor, and if I have cheated anyone, I will pay him back four times as much."

9 Jesus said to him, "Salvation has come to this house today, for this man, also, is a descendant of Abraham. 10 The Son of Man came to seek and to save the lost."

The Parable of the Gold Coins
(Matt. 25.14–30)

11 While the people were listening to this, Jesus

He...could not see Jesus because of the crowd (19.3)

continued and told them a parable. He was now almost
at Jerusalem, and they supposed that the Kingdom
of God was just about to appear. 12 So he said, "There
was once a man of high rank who was going to
a country far away to be made king, after which
he planned to come back home. 13 Before he left, he
called his ten servants and gave them each a gold
coin and told them, 'See what you can earn with
this while I am gone.' 14 Now, his countrymen hated
him, and so they sent messengers after him to say,
'We don't want this man to be our king.'

15 "The man was made king and came back. At

once he ordered his servants to appear before him, in order to find out how much they had earned. 16 The first one came and said, 'Sir, I have earned ten gold coins with the one you gave me.' 17 'Well done,' he said; 'you are a good servant! Since you were faithful in small matters, I will put you in charge of ten cities.' 18 The second servant came and said, 'Sir, I have earned five gold coins with the one you gave me.' 19 To this one he said, 'You will be in charge of five cities.'

20 "Another servant came and said, 'Sir, here is your gold coin; I kept it hidden in a handkerchief. 21 I was afraid of you, because you are a hard man. You take what is not yours and reap what you did not sow.' 22 He said to him, 'You bad servant! I will use your own words to condemn you! You know that I am a hard man, taking what is not mine and reaping what I have not sown. 23 Well, then, why didn't you put my money in the bank? Then I would have received it back with interest when I returned.'

24 "Then he said to those who were standing there, 'Take the gold coin away from him and give it to the servant who has ten coins.' 25 But they said to him, 'Sir, he already has ten coins!' 26 'I tell you,' he replied, 'that to every person who has something, even more will be given; but the person who has nothing, even the little that he has will be taken away from him. 27 Now, as for those enemies of mine who did not want me to be their king, bring them here and kill them in my presence!' "

The Triumphant Approach to Jerusalem
(Matt. 21.1-11; Mark 11.1-11; John 12.12-19)

28 Jesus said this and then went on to Jerusalem ahead of them. 29 As he came near Bethphage and Bethany at the Mount of Olives, he sent two disciples ahead 30 with these instructions: "Go to the village there ahead of you; as you go in, you will find a colt tied up that has never been ridden. Untie it and bring it here. 31 If someone asks you why you are untying it, tell him that the Master x needs it."

x the Master; or its owner.

32 They went on their way and found everything just as Jesus had told them. 33 As they were untying the colt, its owners said to them, "Why are you untying it?"

34 "The Master needs it," they answered, 35 and they took the colt to Jesus. Then they threw their cloaks over the animal and helped Jesus get on. 36 As he rode on, people spread their cloaks on the road.

37 When he came near Jerusalem, at the place where the road went down the Mount of Olives, the large crowd of his disciples began to thank God and praise him in loud voices for all the great things that they had seen: 38 "God bless the king who comes in the name of the Lord! Peace in heaven and glory to God!"

39 Then some of the Pharisees in the crowd spoke to Jesus. "Teacher," they said, "command your disciples to be quiet!"

40 Jesus answered, "I tell you that if they keep quiet, the stones themselves will start shouting."

Jesus Weeps over Jerusalem

41 He came closer to the city, and when he saw it, he wept over it, 42 saying, "If you only knew today what is needed for peace! But now you cannot see it! 43 The time will come when your enemies will surround you with barricades, blockade you, and close in on you from every side. 44 They will completely destroy you and the people within your walls; not a single stone will they leave in its place, because you did not recognize the time when God came to save you!"

Jesus Goes to the Temple
(Matt. 21.12-17; Mark 11.15-19; John 2.13-22)

45 Then Jesus went into the Temple and began to drive out the merchants, 46 saying to them, "It is written in the Scriptures that God said, 'My Temple will be called a house of prayer.' But you have turned it into a hideout for thieves!"

47 Every day Jesus taught in the Temple. The chief priests, the teachers of the Law, and the leaders of the people wanted to kill him, 48 but they could not

find a way to do it, because all the people kept listening to him, not wanting to miss a single word.

The Question about Jesus' Authority
(Matt. 21.23–27; Mark 11.27–33)

20 One day when Jesus was in the Temple teaching the people and preaching the Good News, the chief priests and the teachers of the Law, together with the elders, came ²and said to him, "Tell us, what right have you to do these things? Who gave you this right?"

3 Jesus answered them, "Now let me ask you a question. Tell me, ⁴did John's right to baptize come from God or from man?"

5 They started to argue among themselves, "What shall we say? If we say, 'From God,' he will say, 'Why, then, did you not believe John?' ⁶But if we say 'From man,' this whole crowd here will stone us, because they are convinced that John was a prophet." ⁷So they answered, "We don't know where it came from."

8 And Jesus said to them, "Neither will I tell you, then, by what right I do these things."

The Parable of the Tenants in the Vineyard
(Matt. 21.33–46; Mark 12.1–12)

9 Then Jesus told the people this parable: "There was once a man who planted a vineyard, let it out to tenants, and then left home for a long time. ¹⁰When the time came to gather the grapes, he sent a slave to the tenants to receive from them his share of the harvest. But the tenants beat the slave and sent him back without a thing. ¹¹So he sent another slave; but the tenants beat him also, treated him shamefully, and sent him back without a thing. ¹²Then he sent a third slave; the tenants wounded him, too, and threw him out. ¹³Then the owner of the vineyard said, 'What shall I do? I will send my own dear son; surely they will respect him!' ¹⁴But when the tenants saw him, they said to one another, 'This is the owner's son. Let's kill him, and his property will be ours!' ¹⁵So they threw him out of the vineyard and killed him.

"What, then, will the owner of the vineyard do to the tenants?" Jesus asked. 16 "He will come and kill those men, and hand the vineyard over to other tenants."

When the people heard this, they said, "Surely not!"

17 Jesus looked at them and asked, "What, then, does this scripture mean?

'The stone which the builders rejected as worthless
turned out to be the most important of all.'

18 Everyone who falls on that stone will be cut to pieces; and if that stone falls on someone, it will crush him to dust."

The Question about Paying Taxes
(Matt. 22.15-22; Mark 12.13-17)

19 The teachers of the Law and the chief priests tried to arrest Jesus on the spot, because they knew that he had told this parable against them; but they were afraid of the people. 20 So they looked for an opportunity. They bribed some men to pretend they were sincere, and they sent them to trap Jesus with questions, so that they could hand him over to the authority and power of the Roman Governor. 21 These spies said to Jesus, "Teacher, we know that what you say and teach is right. We know that you pay no attention to a man's status, but teach the truth about God's will for man. 22 Tell us, is it against our Law for us to pay taxes to the Roman Emperor, or not?"

23 But Jesus saw through their trick and said to them, 24 "Show me a silver coin. Whose face and name are these on it?"

"The Emperor's," they answered.

25 So Jesus said, "Well, then, pay the Emperor what belongs to the Emperor, and pay God what belongs to God."

26 There before the people they could not catch him out in anything, so they kept quiet, amazed at his answer.

The Question about Rising from Death
(Matt. 22.23-33; Mark 12.18-27)

27 Then some Sadducees, who say that people will

not rise from death, came to Jesus and said,
²⁸"Teacher, Moses wrote this law for us: 'If a man
dies and leaves a wife but no children, that man's
brother must marry the widow so that they can have
children who will be considered the dead man's children.' ²⁹Once there were seven brothers; the eldest got
married and died without having children. ³⁰Then the
second one married the woman, ³¹and then the third.
The same thing happened to all seven—they died without having children. ³²Last of all, the woman died.
³³Now, on the day when the dead rise to life, whose
wife will she be? All seven of them had married
her."

34 Jesus answered them, "The men and women of
this age marry, ³⁵but the men and women who are
worthy to rise from death and live in the age to
come will not then marry. ³⁶They will be like angels
and cannot die. They are the sons of God, because
they have risen from death. ³⁷And Moses clearly proves
that the dead are raised to life. In the passage about
the burning bush he speaks of the Lord as 'the God
of Abraham, the God of Isaac, and the God of Jacob.'
³⁸He is the God of the living, not of the dead, for
to him all are alive."

39 Some of the teachers of the Law spoke up, "A
good answer, Teacher!" ⁴⁰For they did not dare ask
him any more questions.

The Question about the Messiah
(Matt. 22.41–46; Mark 12.35–37)

41 Jesus asked them, "How can it be said that the
Messiah will be the descendant of David? ⁴²For David
himself says in the book of Psalms,
    'The Lord said to my Lord:
        Sit here on my right
⁴³until I put your enemies as a footstool under your
        feet.'
⁴⁴David called him 'Lord'; how, then, can the Messiah
be David's descendant?"

Jesus Warns against the Teachers of the Law
(Matt. 23.1–36; Mark 12.38–40)

45 As all the people listened to him, Jesus said

to his disciples, 46"Be on your guard against the teachers of the Law, who like to walk about in their long robes and love to be greeted with respect in the market-place; who choose the reserved seats in the synagogues and the best places at feasts; 47who take advantage of widows and rob them of their homes, and then make a show of saying long prayers! Their punishment will be all the worse!"

The Widow's Offering
(Mark 12.41–44)

21 Jesus looked round and saw rich men dropping their gifts in the temple treasury, 2and he also saw a very poor widow dropping in two little copper coins. 3He said, "I tell you that this poor widow put in more than all the others. 4For the others offered their gifts from what they had to spare of their riches; but she, poor as she is, gave all she had to live on."

Jesus Speaks of the Destruction of the Temple
(Matt. 24.1–2; Mark 13.1–2)

5 Some of the disciples were talking about the Temple, how beautiful it looked with its fine stones and the gifts offered to God. Jesus said, 6"All this you see—the time will come when not a single stone here will be left in its place; every one will be thrown down."

Troubles and Persecutions
(Matt. 24.3–14; Mark 13.3–13)

7 "Teacher," they asked, "when will this be? And what will happen in order to show that the time has come for it to take place?"

8 Jesus said, "Be on guard; don't be deceived. Many men, claiming to speak for me, will come and say, 'I am he!' and, 'The time has come!' But don't follow them. 9Don't be afraid when you hear of wars and revolutions; such things must happen first, but they do not mean that the end is near."

10 He went on to say, "Countries will fight each other; kingdoms will attack one another. 11There will be terrible earthquakes, famines, and plagues every-

where; there will be strange and terrifying things coming from the sky. 12 Before all these things take place, however, you will be arrested and persecuted; you will be handed over to be tried in synagogues and be put in prison; you will be brought before kings and rulers for my sake. 13 This will be your chance to tell the Good News. 14 Make up your minds beforehand not to worry about how you will defend yourselves, 15 because I will give you such words and wisdom that none of your enemies will be able to refute or contradict what you say. 16 You will be handed over by your parents, your brothers, your relatives, and your friends; and some of you will be put to death. 17 Everyone will hate you because of me. 18 But not a single hair from your heads will be lost. 19 Stand firm, and you will save yourselves.

Jesus Speaks of the Destruction of Jerusalem
(Matt. 24.15-21; Mark 13.14-19)

20 "When you see Jerusalem surrounded by armies, then you will know that she will soon be destroyed. 21 Then those who are in Judaea must run away to the hills; those who are in the city must leave, and those who are out in the country must not go into the city. 22 For those will be 'The Days of Punishment,' to make all that the Scriptures say come true. 23 How terrible it will be in those days for women who are pregnant and for mothers with little babies! Terrible distress will come upon this land, and God's punishment will fall on this people. 24 Some will be killed by the sword, and others will be taken as prisoners to all countries; and the heathen will trample over Jerusalem until their time is up.

The Coming of the Son of Man
(Matt. 24.29-31; Mark 13.24-27)

25 "There will be strange things happening to the sun, the moon, and the stars. On earth whole countries will be in despair, afraid of the roar of the sea and the raging tides. 26 People will faint from fear as they wait for what is coming over the whole earth, for the powers in space will be driven from their courses. 27 Then the Son of Man will appear, coming in a

cloud with great power and glory. ²⁸When these things begin to happen, stand up and raise your heads, because your salvation is near."

The Lesson of the Fig-Tree
(Matt. 24.32–35; Mark 13.28–31)

29 Then Jesus told them this parable: "Think of the fig-tree and all the other trees. ³⁰When you see their leaves beginning to appear, you know that summer is near. ³¹In the same way, when you see these things happening, you will know that the Kingdom of God is about to come.

32 "Remember that all these things will take place before the people now living have all died. ³³Heaven and earth will pass away, but my words will never pass away.

The Need to Watch

34 "Be on your guard! Don't let yourselves become occupied with too much feasting and drinking and with the worries of this life, or that Day may suddenly catch you ³⁵like a trap. For it will come upon all people everywhere on earth. ³⁶Be on the alert and pray always that you will have the strength to go safely through all those things that will happen and to stand before the Son of Man."

37 Jesus spent those days teaching in the Temple, and when evening came, he would go out and spend the night on the Mount of Olives. ³⁸Early each morning all the people went to the Temple to listen to him.

The Plot against Jesus
(Matt. 26.1–5; Mark 14.1–2; John 11.45–53)

22 The time was near for the Festival of Unleavened Bread, which is called the Passover. ²The chief priests and the teachers of the Law were afraid of the people, and so they were trying to find a way of putting Jesus to death secretly.

Judas Agrees to Betray Jesus
(Matt. 26.14–16; Mark 14.10–11)

3 Then Satan entered Judas, called Iscariot, who was one of the twelve disciples. ⁴So Judas went off

and spoke with the chief priests and the officers of the temple guard about how he could betray Jesus to them. 5They were pleased and offered to pay him money. 6Judas agreed to it and started looking for a good chance to hand Jesus over to them without the people knowing about it.

Jesus Prepares to Eat the Passover Meal
(Matt. 26.17-25; Mark 14.12-21; John 13.21-30)

7 The day came during the Festival of Unleavened Bread when the lambs for the Passover meal were to be killed. 8Jesus sent off Peter and John with these instructions: "Go and get the Passover meal ready for us to eat."

9 "Where do you want us to get it ready?" they asked him.

10 He answered, "As you go into the city, a man carrying a jar of water will meet you. Follow him into the house that he enters, 11and say to the owner of the house: 'The Teacher says to you, Where is the room where my disciples and I will eat the Passover meal?' 12He will show you a large furnished room upstairs, where you will get everything ready."

13 They went off and found everything just as Jesus had told them, and they prepared the Passover meal.

The Lord's Supper
(Matt. 26.26-30; Mark 14.22-26; 1 Cor. 11.23-25)

14 When the hour came, Jesus took his place at the table with the apostles. 15He said to them, "I have wanted so much to eat this Passover meal with you before I suffer! 16For I tell you, I will never eat it until it is given its full meaning in the Kingdom of God."

17 Then Jesus took a cup, gave thanks to God, and said, "Take this and share it among yourselves. 18I tell you that from now on I will not drink this wine until the Kingdom of God comes."

19 Then he took a piece of bread, gave thanks to God, broke it, and gave it to them, saying, "This is my body, which is given for you. Do this in memory of me." 20In the same way, he gave them the cup after

the supper, saying, "This cup is God's new covenant sealed with my blood, which is poured out for you.^{y}

21 "But, look! The one who betrays me is here at the table with me! 22 The Son of Man will die as God has decided, but how terrible for that man who betrays him!"

23 Then they began to ask among themselves which one of them it could be who was going to do this.

The Argument about Greatness

24 An argument broke out among the disciples as to which one of them should be thought of as the greatest. 25 Jesus said to them, "The kings of the pagans have power over their people, and the rulers are called 'Friends of the People.' 26 But this is not the way it is with you; rather, the greatest one among you must be like the youngest, and the leader must be like the servant. 27 Who is greater, the one who sits down to eat or the one who serves him? The one who sits down, of course. But I am among you as one who serves.

28 "You have stayed with me all through my trials; 29 and just as my Father has given me the right to rule, so I will give you the same right. 30 You will eat and drink at my table in my Kingdom, and you will sit on thrones to rule over the twelve tribes of Israel.

Jesus Predicts Peter's Denial
(Matt. 26.31–35; Mark 14.27–31; John 13.36–38)

31 "Simon, Simon! Listen! Satan has received permission to test all of you, to separate the good from the bad, as a farmer separates the wheat from the chaff. 32 But I have prayed for you, Simon, that your faith will not fail. And when you turn back to me, you must strengthen your brothers."

33 Peter answered, "Lord, I am ready to go to prison with you and to die with you!"

34 "I tell you, Peter," Jesus said, "the cock will not crow tonight until you have said three times that you do not know me."

^{y} Some manuscripts do not have the words of Jesus after This is my body in verse 19, and all of verse 20.

Purse, Bag, and Sword

35 Then Jesus asked his disciples, "When I sent you out that time without purse, bag, or shoes, did you lack anything?"

"Not a thing," they answered.

36 "But now," Jesus said, "whoever has a purse or a bag must take it; and whoever has no sword must sell his coat and buy one. 37 For I tell you that the scripture which says, 'He shared the fate of criminals,' must come true about me, because what was written about me is coming true."

38 The disciples said, "Look! Here are two swords, Lord!"

"That is enough!" z he replied.

Jesus Prays on the Mount of Olives
(Matt. 26.36–46; Mark 14.32–42)

39 Jesus left the city and went, as he usually did, to the Mount of Olives; and the disciples went with him. 40 When he arrived at the place, he said to them, "Pray that you will not fall into temptation."

41 Then he went off from them about the distance of a stone's throw and knelt down and prayed. 42 "Father," he said, "if you will, take this cup of suffering away from me. Not my will, however, but your will be done." 43 An angel from heaven appeared to him and strengthened him. 44 In great anguish he prayed even more fervently; his sweat was like drops of blood falling to the ground. a

45 Rising from his prayer, he went back to the disciples and found them asleep, worn out by their grief. 46 He said to them, "Why are you sleeping? Get up and pray that you will not fall into temptation."

The Arrest of Jesus
(Matt. 26.47–56; Mark 14.43–50; John 18.3–11)

47 Jesus was still speaking when a crowd arrived, led by Judas, one of the twelve disciples. He came

z That is enough; or Enough of this.
a Some manuscripts do not have verses 43–44.

up to Jesus to kiss him. [48] But Jesus said, "Judas, is it with a kiss that you betray the Son of Man?"

49 When the disciples who were with Jesus saw what was going to happen, they asked, "Shall we use our swords, Lord?" [50] And one of them struck the High Priest's slave and cut off his right ear.

51 But Jesus said, "Enough of this!" He touched the man's ear and healed him.

52 Then Jesus said to the chief priests and the officers of the temple guard and the elders who had come there to get him, "Did you have to come with swords and clubs, as though I were an outlaw? [53] I was with you in the Temple every day, and you did not try to arrest me. But this is your hour to act, when the power of darkness rules."

Peter Denies Jesus
(Matt. 26.57–58, 69–75; Mark 14.53–54, 66–72; John 18.12–18, 25–27)

54 They arrested Jesus and took him away into the house of the High Priest; and Peter followed at a distance. [55] A fire had been lit in the centre of the courtyard, and Peter joined those who were sitting round it. [56] When one of the servant-girls saw him

This man too was with Jesus! (22.56)

sitting there at the fire, she looked straight at him and said, "This man too was with Jesus!"

57 But Peter denied it, "Woman, I don't even know him!"

58 After a little while a man noticed Peter and said, "You are one of them, too!"

But Peter answered, "Man, I am not!"

59 And about an hour later another man insisted strongly, "There isn't any doubt that this man was with Jesus, because he also is a Galilean!"

60 But Peter answered, "Man, I don't know what you are talking about!"

At once, while he was still speaking, a cock crowed. 61 The Lord turned round and looked straight at Peter, and Peter remembered that the Lord had said to him, "Before the cock crows tonight, you will say three times that you do not know me." 62 Peter went out and wept bitterly.

Jesus Is Mocked and Beaten
(Matt. 26.67–68; Mark 14.65)

63 The men who were guarding Jesus mocked him and beat him. 64 They blindfolded him and asked him, "Who hit you? Guess!" 65 And they said many other insulting things to him.

Jesus Is Brought Before the Council
(Matt. 26.59–66; Mark 14.55–64; John 18.19–24)

66 When day came, the elders, the chief priests, and the teachers of the Law met together, and Jesus was brought before the Council. 67 "Tell us," they said, "are you the Messiah?"

He answered, "If I tell you, you will not believe me; 68 and if I ask you a question, you will not answer. 69 But from now on the Son of Man will be seated on the right of Almighty God."

70 They all said, "Are you, then, the Son of God?"

He answered them, "You say that I am."

71 And they said, "We don't need any witnesses! We ourselves have heard what he said!"

Jesus Is Brought Before Pilate
(Matt. 27.1-2, 11-14; Mark 15.1-5; John 18.28-38)

23 The whole group rose up and took Jesus before Pilate, 2where they began to accuse him: "We caught this man misleading our people, telling them not to pay taxes to the Emperor and claiming that he himself is the Messiah, a king."

3 Pilate asked him, "Are you the king of the Jews?"

"So you say," answered Jesus.

4 Then Pilate said to the chief priests and the crowds, "I find no reason to condemn this man."

5 But they insisted even more strongly, "With his teaching he is starting a riot among the people all through Judaea. He began in Galilee and now has come here."

Jesus Is Sent to Herod

6 When Pilate heard this, he asked, "Is this man a Galilean?" 7When he learnt that Jesus was from the region ruled by Herod, he sent him to Herod, who was also in Jerusalem at that time. 8Herod was very pleased when he saw Jesus, because he had heard about him and had been wanting to see him for a long time. He was hoping to see Jesus perform some miracle. 9So Herod asked Jesus many questions, but Jesus made no answer. 10The chief priests and the teachers of the Law stepped forward and made strong accusations against Jesus. 11Herod and his soldiers mocked Jesus and treated him with contempt; then they put a fine robe on him and sent him back to Pilate. 12On that very day Herod and Pilate became friends; before this they had been enemies.

Jesus Is Sentenced to Death
(Matt. 27.15-26; Mark 15.6-15; John 18.39-19.16)

13 Pilate called together the chief priests, the leaders, and the people, 14and said to them, "You brought this man to me and said that he was misleading the people. Now, I have examined him here in your presence, and I have not found him guilty of any of the crimes you accuse him of. 15Nor did Herod find him guilty, for he sent him back to us. There is

nothing this man has done to deserve death. ¹⁶So
I will have him whipped and let him go." ᵇ

18 The whole crowd cried out, "Kill him! Set
Barabbas free for us!" ¹⁹(Barabbas had been put in
prison for a riot that had taken place in the city,
and for murder.)

20 Pilate wanted to set Jesus free, so he appealed
to the crowd again. ²¹But they shouted back, "Crucify
him! Crucify him!"

22 Pilate said to them the third time, "But what
crime has he committed? I cannot find he has done
anything to deserve death! I will have him whipped
and set him free."

23 But they kept on shouting at the top of their
voices that Jesus should be crucified, and finally their
shouting succeeded. ²⁴So Pilate passed the sentence
on Jesus that they were asking for. ²⁵He set free
the man they wanted, the one who had been put
in prison for riot and murder, and he handed Jesus
over for them to do as they wished.

Jesus Is Crucified
(Matt. 27.32–44; Mark 15.21–32; John 19.17–27)

26 The soldiers led Jesus away, and as they were
going, they met a man from Cyrene named Simon
who was coming into the city from the country. They
seized him, put the cross on him, and made him
carry it behind Jesus.

27 A large crowd of people followed him; among
them were some women who were weeping and wailing
for him. ²⁸Jesus turned to them and said, "Women
of Jerusalem! Don't cry for me, but for yourselves
and your children. ²⁹For the days are coming when
people will say, 'How lucky are the women who never
had children, who never bore babies, who never nursed
them!' ³⁰That will be the time when people will say
to the mountains, 'Fall on us!' and to the hills, 'Hide
us!' ³¹For if such things as these are done when
the wood is green, what will happen when it is dry?"

32 Two other men, both of them criminals, were

ᵇ Some manuscripts add verse 17: At every Passover Festival
Pilate had to set free one prisoner for them (see Mk 15.6).

They...put the cross on him, and made him carry it (23.26)

also led out to be put to death with Jesus. ³³When they came to the place called "The Skull," they crucified Jesus there, and the two criminals, one on his right and the other on his left. ³⁴Jesus said, "Forgive them, Father! They don't know what they are doing." *c*

They divided his clothes among themselves by throwing dice. ³⁵The people stood there watching while the Jewish leaders jeered at him: "He saved others; let him save himself if he is the Messiah whom God has chosen!"

36 The soldiers also mocked him: they came up to him and offered him cheap wine, ³⁷and said, "Save yourself if you are the king of the Jews!"

38 Above him were written these words: "This is the King of the Jews."

39 One of the criminals hanging there hurled insults at him: "Aren't you the Messiah? Save yourself and us!"

40 The other one, however, rebuked him, saying "Don't you fear God? You received the same sentence he did. ⁴¹Ours, however, is only right, because we are getting what we deserve for what we did; but

c *Some manuscripts do not have* Jesus said, "Forgive them, Father! They don't know what they are doing."

he has done no wrong." ⁴²And he said to Jesus, "Remember me, Jesus, when you come as King!"

43 Jesus said to him, "I promise you that today you will be in Paradise with me."

The Death of Jesus
(Matt. 27.45–56; Mark 15.33–41; John 19.28–30)

44 It was about twelve o'clock when the sun stopped shining and darkness covered the whole country until three o'clock; ⁴⁵and the curtain hanging in the Temple was torn in two. ⁴⁶Jesus cried out in a loud voice,

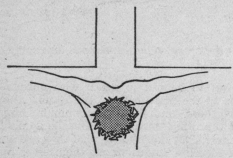

Father! In your hands I place my spirit! (23.46)

"Father! In your hands I place my spirit!" He said this and died.

47 The army officer saw what had happened, and he praised God, saying, "Certainly he was a good man!"

48 When the people who had gathered there to watch the spectacle saw what happened, they all went back home, beating their breasts in sorrow. ⁴⁹All those who knew Jesus personally, including the women who had followed him from Galilee, stood at a distance to watch.

The Burial of Jesus
(Matt. 27.57–61; Mark 15.42–47; John 19.38–42)

50–51 There was a man named Joseph from Arimathea, a town in Judaea. He was a good and honourable man, who was waiting for the coming of the Kingdom of God. Although he was a member of the Council, he had not agreed with their decision and action. •⁵²He went into the presence of Pilate and asked for the body of Jesus. ⁵³Then he took the body down, wrapped it in a linen sheet, and placed it in a tomb which had been dug out of solid rock and which had never been used. ⁵⁴It was Friday, and the Sabbath was about to begin.

55 The women who had followed Jesus from Galilee went with Joseph and saw the tomb and how Jesus' body was placed in it. ⁵⁶Then they went back home and prepared the spices and perfumes for the body.

On the Sabbath they rested, as the Law commanded.

The Resurrection
(Matt. 28.1–10; Mark 16.1–8; John 20.1–10)

24 Very early on Sunday morning the women went to the tomb, carrying the spices they had prepared. ²They found the stone rolled away from the entrance to the tomb, ³so they went in; but they did not find the body of the Lord Jesus. ⁴They stood there puzzled about this, when suddenly two men in bright shining clothes stood by them. ⁵Full of fear, the women bowed down to the ground, as the men said to them, "Why are you looking among the dead for one who is alive? ⁶He is not here; he has been raised. Remember what he said to you while he was in Galilee: ⁷'The Son of Man must be handed over to sinful men, be crucified, and three days later rise to life.' "

8 Then the women remembered his words, ⁹returned from the tomb, and told all these things to the eleven disciples and all the rest. ¹⁰The women were Mary Magdalene, Joanna, and Mary the mother of James; they and the other women with them told these things to the apostles. ¹¹But the apostles thought that what the women said was nonsense, and they did not believe them. ¹²But Peter got up and ran to the tomb; he bent down and saw the linen wrappings but nothing else. Then he went back home amazed at what had happened. *d*

d Some manuscripts do not have verse 12.

He is not here; he has been raised (24.6)

The Walk to Emmaus
(Mark 16.12–13)

13 On that same day two of Jesus' followers were going to a village named Emmaus, about eleven kilometres from Jerusalem, 14 and they were talking to each other about all the things that had happened. 15 As they talked and discussed, Jesus himself drew near and walked along with them; 16 they saw him, but somehow did not recognize him. 17 Jesus said to them, "What are you talking about to each other, as you walk along?"

They stood still, with sad faces. 18 One of them, named Cleopas, asked him, "Are you the only visitor in Jerusalem who doesn't know the things that have been happening there these last few days?"

19 "What things?" he asked.

"The things that happened to Jesus of Nazareth," they answered. "This man was a prophet and was considered by God and by all the people to be powerful in everything he said and did. 20 Our chief priests and rulers handed him over to be sentenced to death, and he was crucified. 21 And we had hoped that he would be the one who was going to set Israel free! Besides all that, this is now the third day since it happened. [22] Some of the women of our group surprised us; they went at dawn to the tomb, [23] but could not find his body. They came back saying they had seen a vision of angels who told them that he is alive. [24] Some of our group went to the tomb and found it exactly as the women had said, but they did not see him."

25 Then Jesus said to them, "How foolish you are, how slow you are to believe everything the prophets said! [26] Was it not necessary for the Messiah to suffer these things and then to enter his glory?" [27] And Jesus explained to them what was said about himself in all the Scriptures, beginning with the books of Moses and the writings of all the prophets.

28 As they came near the village to which they were going, Jesus acted as if he were going farther; [29] but they held him back, saying, "Stay with us; the day is almost over and it is getting dark." So he went in to stay with them. [30] He sat down to eat with them, took the bread, and said the blessing; then he broke the bread and gave it to them. [31] Then their eyes were opened and they recognized him, but he disappeared from their sight. [32] They said to each other, "Wasn't it like a fire burning in us when he talked to us on the road and explained the Scriptures to us?"

33 They got up at once and went back to Jerusalem, where they found the eleven disciples gathered together with the others [34] and saying, "The Lord is risen indeed! He has appeared to Simon!"

35 The two then explained to them what had happened on the road, and how they had recognized the Lord when he broke the bread.

Jesus Appears to His Disciples
(Matt. 28.16–20; Mark 16.14–18; John 20.19–23; Acts 1.6–8)

36 While the two were telling them this, suddenly the Lord himself stood among them and said to them, "Peace be with you." [e]

37 They were terrified, thinking that they were seeing

---

[e] Some manuscripts do not have and said to them, "Peace be with you."

a ghost. 38But he said to them, "Why are you alarmed? Why are these doubts coming up in your minds? 39Look at my hands and my feet, and see that it is I myself. Feel me, and you will know, for a ghost doesn't have flesh and bones, as you can see I have."

40 He said this and showed them his hands and his feet.ᶠ 41They still could not believe, they were so full of joy and wonder; so he asked them, "Have you anything here to eat?" 42They gave him a piece of cooked fish, 43which he took and ate in their presence.

44 Then he said to them, "These are the very things I told you about while I was still with you: everything written about me in the Law of Moses, the writings of the prophets, and the Psalms had to come true."

45 Then he opened their minds to understand the Scriptures, 46and said to them, "This is what is written: the Messiah must suffer and must rise from death three days later, 47and in his name the message about repentance and the forgiveness of sins must be preached to all nations, beginning in Jerusalem. 48You are witnesses of these things. 49And I myself will send upon you what my Father has promised. But you must wait in the city until the power from above comes down upon you."

Jesus Is Taken up to Heaven
(Mark 16.19-20; Acts 1.9-11)

50 Then he led them out of the city as far as Bethany, where he raised his hands and blessed them. 51As he was blessing them, he departed from them and was taken up into heaven.ᵍ 52They worshipped him and went back into Jerusalem, filled with great joy, 53and spent all their time in the Temple giving thanks to God.

ᶠSome manuscripts do not have verse 40.
ᵍSome manuscripts do not have and was taken up into heaven.

Some stories from the Good News

page

Passages to read when you are feeling:

Passages to read when you are wondering about:

THERE'S MORE GOOD NEWS TO READ

After
**Good News
told by Luke**

Read
**Good News
New Testament**

75p Post Free*

With index, word list and 100 illustrations

To: The Bible Society
146 Queen Victoria Street, London EC4V 4BX
or
7 Hampton Terrace, Edinburgh EH12 5XU

Please send me **POST FREE** a **GOOD NEWS NEW TESTAMENT**. I enclose a cheque/P.O. for 75p

NAME: MR/MRS/MISS_____

ADDRESS:_____

_____

POSTCODE:_____

*While stocks last